Cambridge Elements

Elements in Politics and Society in Southeast Asia
edited by
Edward Aspinall
Australian National University
Meredith L. Weiss
University at Albany, SUNY

MYANMAR

A Political Lexicon

Nick Cheesman
Australian National University, Canberra

Shaftesbury Road, Cambridge CB2 8EA, United Kingdom

One Liberty Plaza, 20th Floor, New York, NY 10006, USA

477 Williamstown Road, Port Melbourne, VIC 3207, Australia

314–321, 3rd Floor, Plot 3, Splendor Forum, Jasola District Centre,
New Delhi – 110025, India

103 Penang Road, #05–06/07, Visioncrest Commercial, Singapore 238467

Cambridge University Press is part of Cambridge University Press & Assessment,
a department of the University of Cambridge.

We share the University's mission to contribute to society through the pursuit of
education, learning and research at the highest international levels of excellence.

www.cambridge.org
Information on this title: www.cambridge.org/9781009454339

DOI: 10.1017/9781108565523

First published 2023

A catalogue record for this publication is available from the British Library

ISBN 978-1-009-45433-9 Hardback
ISBN 978-1-108-46474-1 Paperback
ISSN 2515-2998 (online)
ISSN 2515-298X (print)

Myanmar

A Political Lexicon

Elements in Politics and Society in Southeast Asia

DOI: 10.1017/9781108565523
First published online: November 2023

Nick Cheesman
Australian National University, Canberra

Author for correspondence: Nick Cheesman, nick.cheesman@anu.edu.au

Abstract: *Myanmar: A Political Lexicon* is a critical inquiry into how words animate politics. Across sixteen entries, the lexicon stages dialogues about political speech and action in this country at the nexus of South, East and Southeast Asia. This Element offers readers venues in which to consider the history and contingency of ideas like power, race, patriarchy and revolution. Contention over these and other ideas, it shows, does not reflect the political world in which Myanmar's people live – it realises it.

Keywords: Myanmar, Burma, politics, meaning, lexicon

ISBNs: 9781009454339 (HB), 9781108464741 (PB), 9781108565523 (OC)
ISSNs: 2515-2998 (online), 2515-298X (print)

Contents

A Political Lexicon: How Come?   1

1 Politics   10

2 Power   13

3 Dictatorship   16

4 Federalism   18

5 Sovereignty   21

6 Citizen   24

7 Race   27

8 Buddhism   30

9 Genocide   34

10 Impunity   37

11 Interrogation   39

12 Revolution   41

13 Reform   45

14 Development   48

15 Patriarchy   53

16 Freedom   56

References   59

A Political Lexicon: How Come?

Myanmar is a country dense with political ideas and crowded with political actors. If this were not obvious before 1 February 2021, when the country's military again seized its government, it was almost immediately afterward. The quality of the resistance that people in Myanmar showed to the takeover was remarkable. For over two months, acephalous protests ran up and down the country's length. Throngs of bodies and emotions enveloped Yangon, Mandalay, and provincial towns and cities around the country. People assembled in a festive atmosphere, celebrating Daw Aung San Suu Kyi, whose National League for Democracy had overwhelmingly won a general election the year before and who was about to lead a new legislature. They called for her release, along with that of hundreds, then thousands, of other political prisoners from her political party and others, not to mention many from state agencies.

With their numbers growing, assembled demonstrators began to challenge notions of political order in Myanmar that, in the three-quarters of a century since the country pulled free from the disintegrating British Empire in 1948, have never been settled. Even before soldiers and paramilitaries started systematically shooting protesters dead, abducting people from their homes and profaning corpses, demands for the recall of the semi-elected legislature were supplemented, and then supplanted, by calls to overthrow the military state itself. As soldiers, paramilitary police and their proxies shot, assaulted and humiliated demonstrators, civilians who yet took to the streets inverted the relationship between themselves and their adversaries. They denounced the soldiers and paramilitary cops who approached them as robbers of sovereign power, not guardians of it. They did this in chants and jeers and by holding placards that read like:

အာဏာလု စစ်အစိုးရအလိုမရှိ / Down with usurper military government!

စစ်သူပုန်များ ဖြုတ်ချရေး ဦးအရေး / Our aim: overthrow the military rebels!

ဖက်ဆစ်စစ်တပ် အမြစ်ဖြတ် / Cut the fascist army at the roots!

Taken out of context, these might seem like expressions of anger that could be directed towards military government anywhere – evocative of what people in those assembled crowds felt, but not revealing much of political thought and action. This lexicon rests on the opposite premise. The countless aphorisms, poems and songs heaping ridicule on the army and its running dogs, *sitkwe*, after the February coup did much more than merely convey contempt. They theorised forms of power relations which were alternatives to the ones on which Myanmar's military insists.

How? Well, in conditions in which army officers claim an exclusive and unmediated right to defend sovereign power from the nation's enemies, protesters inverted the relation of soldiers to sovereignty. They labelled the Tatmadaw (Defence Services) a rebel army, *thubôn sitdat*. In this one usage, Myanmar citizens, political activists and enemies of its armed forces turned the political world upside down. They denied the military any exclusive right to guard sovereignty and assigned that right to themselves. In this way, they upended their relations with soldiers sent to kill, capture and humiliate them. *Thubôn sitdat* is not a glorious institution. It is a murderous gang, a rabble. The only right thing to do is to fight it.

What about condemnation of the army as fascist? Isn't this just a smear borrowed from the language of social movements abroad? No, it is not that at all. It is an allusion, but not to fascism as an ideal type, nor to the historical experience of fascism in Europe that gives the term substance in English. Instead, it registers the historical narrative of fascism in Myanmar (then called Burma) during the Second World War and, with this, the fascism of historical myth against which people back then united in struggle. That is to say, 'fascist army' is less about the qualities of the army itself than it is about those of its anti-fascist opponents. It does not matter whether the army meets criteria for a formal definition of fascism or not, and to cast around for such criteria would be to miss the point. 'Fascist' here is a negative descriptor, a placeholder; '*anti*-fascist', the term implied by it, is its productive opponent. The epithet 'fascist army', then, places today's struggle in an historical lineage to which people can refer and from which they can draw as they organise, innovate, form alliances, press claims and together make the political world in which they live.

The language people use with one another, the meanings they infer and the assemblies they form to hear and be heard do not reflect the political world; they realise it. When language is revolutionary, it endows those who use it with a power of public speech that they would not otherwise have. It provides them, as the historian William Sewell (1980: 201) has written, with the 'power to redefine the moral and social world'. This is why the words with which people are made political subjects and through which they interpret and remake political subjectivity deserve attention.

But which words should get attention and why? That question brings me to the design of this lexicon: to the approach that I took to researching and writing it; and the choices I have made when deciding which words to select for its entries. In the remainder of this introduction I explain these. I begin with the principles that guided its design, its background and its rationale. I conclude with three contributions I hope it can make to the understanding of politics in

Myanmar. The remainder of the Element consists of the lexicon's sixteen entries, followed by recommended readings for each.

Myanmar: A Political Lexicon is a critical inquiry into political usages and into the times and places that these usages have animated politics in the mainland Southeast Asian country that is its site of inquiry. The rubrics for its entries serve as a series of lexical prompts. Though they are followed by dictionary definitions, the entries sketch lexical relations. In this respect, they depart from the keywords approach that Raymond Williams (1983) made famous. In that approach, the author's concern remains with the words themselves as semantic units (see Fassin and Das 2021). In this lexicon, the selected words do not mirror meanings. They are entries, or openings, into possible dialogues. It follows that, unlike certain terminological works on Myanmar (e.g., Seekins 2006), the lexicon does not aim at completeness. It makes no pretence of comprehensiveness. Its entries are few. They decide nothing. What they offer, in combination, is a venue in which to stage relations between certain words, to see what they do or do not do politically, how they coexist and how they might otherwise be.

Williams says that, although they might seem somewhat arbitrary, his keywords forced themselves onto his attention because the problems of their meanings seemed to be bound up with the problems the words were being used to discuss. The words caught his eye and ear because they were doing things that mattered to culture and society. Like him, I have selected terms that have troubled me personally. These are what Craig Reynolds (2014) has called 'worry words'. It is because they are worrying that they have pressed me to think harder about concepts and categories. And it is because I have worried about them that they have from time to time revealed some things and led me to think about some others.

As conditions have changed in Myanmar, so has what has worried me. However, my basic intuition has not. Rather than try to sum things up or write a report based on the contents of source materials, my aim throughout has been to choose words with which to make the lexicon political in two senses: one, in the sense that it is about politics in Myanmar; the other, in that it is itself political, because it stages a dialogue between the terms it contains and invites a conversation between me the author and you the reader.

Unlike Williams, I never intended to tease out the entries' semantic histories. The lexicon's method is, as Carol Gluck (2009) writes of her and Anna Tsing's jointly edited *Words in Motion*, situated in time and place. But what does that mean for the writing of this lexicon? Throughout, I have been guided by three principles (drawing on Bernstein, Ophir and Stoler 2018). The first goes back to criteria for selection of entries. It was that the lexicon should comprise an admixture of conventional political usages, in Burmese and English (like the entries for **Dictatorship** and **Federalism**), while including words that are not necessarily political (like those for **Interrogation** and **Buddhism**). My goal was to query assumptions about politics and the political in Myanmar so as to open words to inquiry that they might not otherwise get.

A second principle was that the lexicon should remain attentive to how translation itself is a political concept (Lezra 2018). The politics of translation in or from Burmese is unlike translation in or from English (Cheesman 2021). In English *trans-lation*, something is moved from one place to another. A word or phrase is transferred. It is picked up and dropped off as if by taxi. In Burmese, on the other hand, words translate by rebounding from one language to another. They are not transferred so much as they are negotiated and reinterpreted. I have tried to evoke something of this back-and-forth, which is why readers may find that the entries have an open-ended quality. Their inconclusiveness is not an oversight. It is for the reader to decide what comes next.

The third principle was that the lexicon should reach for big ideas about politics without trying to grasp them in all their bigness and, likewise, that it should look into small details of politics without getting entangled in them. Following this principle, the lexicon is neither a work of general theory nor a compendium of facts and figures. It is a series of exchanges in which ideas that words connote or denote are called to account. A principle annexed to this one was that the lexicon should be unencumbered by jargon and minutiae, to make it easy to read – but not so easy that it can be read hastily. The entries are short, but they ask the reader to pause and question the truths that words in everyday life convey as self-evident and in need of no further justification. They invite the reader, I hope, into a conversation that follows from what are, for me, by now three decades of conversations that I have had about the many meanings of politics in Myanmar.

It has been written that the past is a foreign country. If so, its foreignness may prove to have been an advantage for me when writing this lexicon. I sense Myanmar's past as I do my own, but I can only apprehend it as something distant and foreign, familiar but unsettling. When I first took interest in what was happening in Myanmar, as an undergraduate at the University of Melbourne, the news reports were of soldiers who had seized government. Myanmar – or, as we insisted on calling it, Burma (see Metro 2011) – had had a student-led uprising in 1988 that brought down the Burma Socialist Programme Party state, but this, as in 2021, ended bloodily. I read Bertil Lintner's (1990) account of it, found out about the country's history of colonial invasion and occupation, and learned about how Burma was, from the moment of its political independence in 1948, beset by strife (see Charney 2009).

I got hold of human rights groups' newsletters, which circulated through the offices of the trades hall. These documented atrocities in the country's highlands and told of half a century of civil war and 'the politics of ethnicity' (Smith 1991).

In Thailand I met people documenting state violence and read first-person narratives of political struggle and resistance (e.g., Aye Saung 1989). I volunteered at a refugee camp on the border with Myanmar, where I learned the rudiments of Burmese – though it was not until later that I went to Yangon (or Rangoon) to study the language in earnest. The army was pursuing armed enemies in Myanmar's highlands and frontiers. It pushed hard against parts of the border with Thailand and China, and it cut deals with armed groups claiming sovereignty over certain subnational territories and the people, creatures and things in them. Para-states like the Karen National Union, which governed the camp where I lived and worked, splintered. Members of a breakaway group in 1997 and 1998 burned the camp down.

In the lowlands the State Law and Order Restoration Council that had usurped power in 1988 repressed all unarmed political opponents. Dissidents went underground. Many fled abroad. The Council locked Aung San Suu Kyi in her house; members of her party, in an archipelago of prisons old and new. Meanwhile, in the name of development, it welcomed capitalists from China, Korea, Japan and other parts of Southeast Asia – Singapore and Thailand in particular. International sanctions and bad press kept non-Asian capital away for a time, though profits from petroleum and natural gas brought multinationals like Total and Unocal. Peri-urban industrial zones contained few factories and many weeds. The country remained agricultural. The junta continued to impose socialist-style quotas on farmers, with which to acquire grains and pulses for redistribution to public servants and for international sale. Hundreds of thousands of young men and women went abroad in search of work – in the fisheries and canneries of Thailand, in the construction sites of Singapore and Abu Dhabi, and in merchant vessels criss-crossing the Indian and Pacific Oceans.

The military insisted that it would govern temporarily. This was necessary, it said, to prepare for the 'discipline flourishing' multiparty democracy under a new constitution to come. It suspended its constitution-drafting convention in 1996 and reconfigured itself the following year as the State Peace and Development Council. Work on the draft constitution resumed in 2003, and it passed through a pantomime referendum in 2008. The military Council indicated that it was now ready to consider electoral politics. One of its constitutional provisos was that its soldiers would occupy a quarter of the seats in the new union legislature. The legislature itself would occupy a grandiose complex that was the centrepiece of Myanmar's newly erected high-modernist answer to Brasilia, Canberra and Islamabad: Naypyidaw.

In 2011 the military's own Union Solidarity and Development Party took government via a tightly controlled election held the year before. The premier of the outgoing junta, General Thein Sein, became president. He proved to be adept at forging an elite pact with Aung San Suu Kyi, bringing her and her National League for Democracy onside while keeping the military committed to partial withdrawal from government and administration of a sort that would not, at least in the short term, threaten its core economic and political interests. As a result, Suu Kyi and forty other members of her party entered the union legislature in a by-election in 2012, right on cue for the anti-Muslim violence that traversed the country that year and the next.

The rest is the recent past, though no less foreign for that. The National League for Democracy swept the 2015 election, forming government in 2016 a quarter-century after the military first denied it the right to do so. In 2020 it won even more seats than it did in 2015 – despite, or perhaps because of, the army's genocidal campaign against Rohingya in the north of Rakhine State, which the League did nothing to try to stop and international criticism of which Aung San Suu Kyi deflected. But if genocidal violence did not cost the League any votes and advantaged a few minor parties, like the Arakan National Party, then it came at a cost to others. Many that had hoped to pick up small numbers of seats representing particular constituencies went away disgruntled, blaming campaign restrictions due to the coronavirus pandemic and major party trickery for their poor results.

Even before the vote, military spokesmen had indicated that they would not acquiesce to another resounding National League for Democracy victory. Egged on by resentful minor party leaders, the military and the Union Solidarity and Development Party lodged a slew of complaints. One military spokesman made the extraordinary claim that the veracity of 8.6 million votes out of around 27 million was in doubt (the Union Election Commission rejected the claim). After the soldiers who occupied one-quarter of the seats in the union legislature and their allies failed to get a special session called to debate alleged voter fraud, their commander, Senior General Min Aung Hlaing, threatened to act. He gave no time or opportunities to negotiate. He had already initiated his plan. The day that the new legislature was due to sit, soldiers detained President U Win Myint. One of Win Myint's deputies, a former army officer, took his place. He signed the order for a state of emergency with which to hand government to the military, which established the State Administrative Council.

Then came the protests. They cut across class, religious, linguistic, occupational, cultural and gendered lines. They were strongest among unions formed by working people in state-owned industries, in city quarters where charismatic young leaders inspired residents to fight back, and in peri-urban areas whose occupants had had enough of decades of dispossession and oppression at the hands of Myanmar's military and its lackeys. They continued until participants could no longer bear the gunfire and systematic, performed atrocities that they met in March and April. Then protests gave way to what has become a protracted revolutionary situation (see El-Ghobashy 2021; Lawson 2019; Tilly 1993). New defensive armed groups, concentrated in upper Myanmar but extending into Yangon and other lower regions of the country, first proliferated and then in parts consolidated. The National Unity Government that in April formed in lieu of the Naypyidaw legislature initially seemed an unlikely contender but then showed itself to be a viable alternative to the military. However, the military state did not collapse. The State Administrative Council, like the State Law and Order Restoration Council and the State Peace and Development Council before it, succeeded in containing politics via the one method for dealing with them that Myanmar's military has mastered: their prevention.

This situation ruled out any further research for the lexicon in Myanmar. Prior to it, before the coronavirus pandemic, in 2018 I had held twenty-five discussions with lawyers, legislators, political activists, human rights defenders, serving and retired university professors, Buddhist monks and fellow researchers about what words they would include in such a political lexicon and why. I collated their recommendations and also collected and read print news media. Over three months I did a simple content analysis of the titles of articles in the news sections of then-popular domestic newspapers (*Daily Eleven*, *The Voice*, *The Standard*, *7 Day News*). In 2019 I carried out additional content analysis of Burmese-language titles in periodicals held at the National Library of Australia, where I consulted monographs and edited volumes, alongside those in my personal library. Later that year I went through newly published Burmese books at Kyoto University.

Since February 2021 my research for the lexicon has been in the manner of an ongoing dialogue with colleagues and students. I have consulted Burmese-language news websites (BBC Burmese Service, Mizzima, Myanmar Now), listened to podcasts (Insight Myanmar, Myanmar Musings, Myanmar Revolutionary Tales), watched videos, and reviewed photographs, statements and memes on platform media (e.g., Facebook pages of people's defence forces and interim university councils), organisational webpages (e.g., the Assistance Association for Political Prisoners, the National Unity Government), military state media and websites, briefing papers and reports issued by researchers, and personal correspondence.

Most entries in the lexicon start with a definition from the standard *Myanmar–English Dictionary* compiled by the Myanmar Language Commission (1998). In the case of the first entry, for example, this is '*naingnganye* / n politics'.

The purpose of including these dictionary entries is not, as indicated, to insist on an authoritative meaning. It is to provide a convenient Romanised version or versions of the Burmese word or words relevant to each entry at its outset. And it is to give a sense of which words appear to have, in the dictionary compilers' view, stability in meaning when moving between Burmese and English, as in 'dictatorship', and which do not, as in 'power'.

A few of the entries begin with English definitions from the *Shorter Oxford English Dictionary* (2007) rather than with Burmese ones. The reason for this is that their Burmese equivalents are not, to my mind, inviting of the type of dialogue to which the entries aspire. They are stilted and rather awkward translations. This is not to imply that all political words that are translated or transplanted from English and other languages are uninteresting or unimportant to the vernacular. As Tamas Wells (2021) and Matthew Walton (2017) have shown, the Burmese *dimogarezi*, for instance, is not a thin veneer on an English or French or Latin or Greek word for democracy. Burmese *dimogarezi* is culturally, historically and linguistically distinctive. We are liable to misunderstand what people in Myanmar say about democracy if all we try to do is find points of correspondence between their *dimogarezi* and our democracy. The same goes for all of the entries in this lexicon, regardless of whether they begin with Burmese or English definitions.

Burmese and English are the two languages with explicit stakes in this lexicon. They are not the only two languages with stakes in Myanmar's politics. The country is home to a mind-boggling diversity of languages. A lot of minority languages have well-established political vocabularies, especially those languages adopted and taught by armed groups in the country's frontier areas, like Mon and Sgaw Karen (see, e.g., South and Lall 2016). The attention that this lexicon pays to Burmese and English does not imply that other vernaculars do not matter. However, an attempt to write a political lexicon that would consider multiple language users and sources in Myanmar would have called for a different research design, working towards different goals from this one (see, by way of one example, Ball et al. 2007).

Following the dictionary extract or extracts with which each of the sixteen entries begins is a short quote or proverb. These gesture to the politics of the word in question, its translation or both, by way of a metaphor or proposal or argument about its use.

The entries are not alphabetically ordered, but they are not arranged arbitrarily either. They are, as I have been at pains to point out, performing and inviting dialogue. Certain entries talk to one another; others, across one another. There is no reason to read them in the order they appear, since they are not a concatenated series but a venue, a place for coming together. Readers can choose to participate in their dialogues or move on. They can enter as they please and leave as they choose.

To assist readers who find their own ways through what follows, each time one of the words for the entries in the lexicon (other than the word with which that entry is concerned) appears it is in **bold**. Readers might use these words as cues for other entries to visit, or they may find another way to get about. A few places in the lexicon contain parenthetical recommendations to look at another entry, where these relate directly to the topic discussed.

The lexicon has no designated exit, no conclusion. Instead it ends with short lists of recommended further readings, organised by entry. These lists follow the bibliographic references for this introduction. As with the entries in the lexicon themselves, many more works might have been included in these lists. Readers might find some of them in Andrew Selth's (2018) bibliography of Burma studies or in the Online Burma Library (https://burmalibrary.org). For readers of Burmese, an indicative list of references follows the further reading lists.

Throughout the lexicon, with the exception of proper nouns, the transcription of Burmese follows the Romanisation System for Burmese, BGN/PCGN 1970 Agreement. This includes the dictionary definitions of the Myanmar Language Commission (which uses a different system). The BGN is a crude system that groups similar-sounding Burmese consonants and vowels together and disregards tonal markers. But it has the advantage of being simple to use and easy to read. Names of people and places follow popularised spellings.

What can a small lexicon contribute to our understanding of politics in Myanmar? What can it say or do in an era of revolution? To these questions, I have three responses with which to conclude these preliminary remarks. The first is that, by attending to how political values are negotiated and transformed through words and deeds, talk and action, I hope this book can be a place for thinking and talking about politics in Myanmar differently from works that try to follow all that talk and action. In tumultuous times it is hard to keep up. There is always something going on. Attention to how words are used, to their valences and histories, to their relations to other words and to power can help us to think when it is hard to get a grip on things. The important thing is to resist the urge to pile up facts – to describe new events and add data as if the accumulation of these will automatically aid understanding. As Lisa Wedeen (2019) has shown in her work on Syria, the opposite can be the case. Undoubtedly, without facts it is not possible to interpret events; however, accumulation of facts not guided by purpose or informed by theory is unproductive, if not counterproductive. I have written this lexicon against that impulse.

The second related contribution that a lexical approach to political meaning-making can make is to show how our interpretations of the political world shape that world and the interpretations that comprise it (see Blakely 2020). The lexicon itself interprets a vernacular world of politics in Myanmar. It does not describe it. It is not a lens onto that world. It is a series of entries into it. It communicates with it. It recounts political practices, not with the goal of providing, on its pages, faithful likenesses but with the objective of producing trustworthy interpretations. There are, after all, no likenesses to be had. There are only more or less trustworthy interpretations of other interpretations of political facts. In this way the lexicon enfolds with all those other interpretations of politics in Myanmar that I have read and heard and discussed and considered.

The third contribution I think this political lexicon makes is that it resists hopelessness. Cynics multiply in dark times. For them, there is no point in opposing dictatorship. Dictators get their way and the vulnerable suffer if people resist, they say. Violence is never the solution, some well-meaning principled folks argue, implying that those who opt to use violence in self-defence are, with their attackers, blameworthy when it intensifies. Others talk knowingly of failed states and military stalemates, as if revolutionary situations were like chess games. Though not every one of the lexicon's entries is hopeful, I have written it against such expressions of futility. Its premise contains my hope. Political ideas flourish in times of conflict and change because there is cause to be hopeful. And where they flourish, there is.

1 Politics

နိုင်ငံရေး / naingnganye / n politics.

Politics are like puppetry, or walking with a stick. *– Burmese saying*

Politics, *naingnganye*, pronounced *naing-gan-ye*, are matters, *-ye*, of a state or polity, *naingngan* or *nainggan*. This denotation chimes with an old-fashioned way of talking about politics, that where a state or polity exists, politics do; conversely, no state or polity, no politics. But like the idea of the state in English, *nainggan* connotes different things. These complicate the idea of the polity in Myanmar and of its politics.

Take the 2008 Constitution of Myanmar, which anticipated the political **reform** of the 2010s. Compare its two versions, Burmese and English. The comparison reveals a number of shifts in usage. In English, *nainggan*, or formally, for Myanmar, the elevated *naingngandaw*, or *nainggandaw*, designates in its first chapter the basic principles of the 'union' and in its second the 'state' structure. 'The sovereign **power** of the Union [*naingngandaw*]', the constitution at its outset runs, 'is derived from the citizens and is in force in the entire country [*naingngandaw*]' (section 4). At its other end, the constitution in chapter 13 refers to the 'state' (*naingngandaw*) flag and the 'national' (*naingngandaw*) anthem.

Naingngan (or *naingngandaw*), then, is at play in different fields of meaning. It does different things, depending on whether politics are imagined as matters of the state or nation, country or union; whether they are constituted by citizens or constitutive of them. Politics as *naingganye* refer to the state but do not correspond to it. The state is a site of political action but not a container for it. Political affairs spill all over the place.

For Myanmar's military, spillage makes politics problematic. Its tasks are to prevent and contain spills – to insist that the state is, in fact, the container in which politics must be conducted and that the military alone can define the limits of the state and of those activities that are properly political. Its theories and methods have varied. The Revolutionary Council (1962 to 1974) and the Burma Socialist Programme Party states (1974 to 1988), each of which was commanded by the country's prototypical dictator, General Ne Win, made monopoly claims on what was political. To participate in politics legitimately, citizens had to join the Party programme. This meant being a member of a mass organisation under state leadership or otherwise contributing to the new socialist economic system.

After the programme met with nationwide protest, the Party collapsed in 1988, and a new junta, the State Law and Order Restoration Council (1988 to 1997; reconstituted as the State Peace and **Development** Council from 1997 to 2011), tried containment through electoral party politics. In the 1990 general election the National League for Democracy, led by Aung San Suu Kyi, charismatic daughter of the country's independence hero, trounced the military's National Unity Party (in Burmese, the 'National **Race**' Unity Party). The military learned from this experience that if politics were like proverbial arts of puppetry then these were practical arts it had not mastered. Politics, it turned out, were harder to handle than puppets and walking sticks. And what the military could not keep its hands on, it would not allow.

The military now prohibited politics, first by locking away Aung San Suu Kyi, as well as leading members of her political party and assorted others, for the better part of the next two decades; second, by making a mockery of politics themselves. Its officers delineated national politics, *amyotha naingganye*, from party politics, *padi naingganye*. The former, they said, were the proper affairs of state in which they were duty-bound to participate. These were for the greater good. They were matters of state **sovereignty**, racial solidarity and territorial integrity. Over these the military would have the final say. This is a notion of politics as command. There is no dialogue, no meeting of minds or exchange of views. Nor is any invited. The active exchange of ideas is unwelcome. Dialogue, in the military's scheme, is an attribute of party politics. Those are small-minded affairs that occupy the attention of people who would, whether they know it or not, ruin the country. National politics are the military's bulwark against that possible outcome of anything aberrantly political.

National politics are formless and aimless. Though they have the appearance of a structure and a set of objectives in the military's three national causes – non-disintegration of the Union; non-disintegration of national solidarity, which is to say, the solidarity of national races; and perpetuation of **sovereignty** – these are nothing other than a restatement of what any sovereign state stands for. Existential threats to territory, authority and **sovereignty** are repugnant to all existing states. All states circumscribe the possibilities for political action. It is in how these threats are formulated and circumscribed that states differ. Where those threats are located in the practice of politics itself, the only thing left to do is to prevent people from thinking and acting politically.

Consequently, from the election in 1990 to the next in 2010 the struggle between Myanmar's military and its political opponents was not a political struggle in the sense of one fought for political **power**. It was a struggle by one side to redefine politics absent of political thought or action; by others, to keep politics alive. The struggle went on in political party gatherings, for as long as those were permitted, in public protests and in the closed-door trials of dissidents. It went on in myriad other places and ways. People in Myanmar, like people living under politically repressive conditions elsewhere, came up with strategies to undermine or mock or bypass military strictures, many of which constituted forms of political resistance, though they were not spoken of in this way. People wrote and talked about politics elliptically. Anyone who was not overtly political avoided speaking about *naingganye* and professed disinterest in them. Better to leave something unsaid than to say something that you might later regret.

Politics did not magically reappear when the military next tried its hand at a general election in 2010. The junta kept Aung San Suu Kyi locked in her house and thousands of her party's members and their affiliates in jails around the country. In 2011 it ushered the last premier of the military junta, General Thein Sein, into the presidency. It delivered the military's Union Solidarity and **Development** Party the bulk of seats in the first union legislature. Its representatives met with uniformed soldiers there. The latter occupied a quarter of the legislature, not as representatives of any constituency but in the name of national politics. Thereafter, the military released Suu Kyi and her party leadership from captivity.

Aung San Suu Kyi and her party members contested and won nearly all available constituencies in a 2012 by-election. She went on to chair the legislature's rule of law committee and by 2014 was campaigning for the next general election. In 2015 the National League for Democracy won over 57 per cent of the vote for the union legislature and 78 per cent of the elected seats – still over 59 per cent of the total seats, including the military's bloc. It was a huge victory and an unequivocal rejection of the military and its affiliates. Suu Kyi, constitutionally blocked from the presidency because she had married and raised children with a non-Myanmar national, instead took the supra-constitutional role of state counsellor and in 2016 effectively became head of government.

With the return of politics, people found their voices and formed new institutions for political action. They assembled in order to be seen and have their claims heard. By the early 2010s not a day went by without, somewhere in Myanmar, peasants blocking a road to demand that land taken from them in the name of **development** be returned or workers occupying a factory compound to insist that they be paid more and that conditions be improved. Buddhist monks came together and called on laypeople to defend their religion and **race** against Muslims. Representatives of armed groups occupying frontier areas gathered in conference halls to negotiate ceasefires and discuss the prospects for **federalism**. Politics started spilling all over the place again. The **citizen** was back. **Power** was once more, so to speak, up for grabs. Or was it?

2 Power

အာဏာ / ana / n power; authority. [Pali ana]
ဩဇာ / awza / n … 3 power; authority; influence (as in အသံ ~ , ~ တိတ္ထမ [the voice of ~, exceeding ~]). …

Awza, as distinct from *ana,* 'permeates'. – *Gustaaf Houtman,* Mental Culture in Burmese Crisis Politics

In Burmese, two short words usefully convey ideas of political power. Both have Indic roots in South Asian statecraft. The first is *ana*. Politically speaking, *ana* is a source of commands that are obeyed because they are issued in the form of maxims backed by force. *Ana* is, as Gustaaf Houtman once observed, centralised power: the power of **dictatorship**, the power of **sovereignty**. It is power represented in organisational charts of authorised decision-makers, *ana-baing*, who by virtue of office possess a quantum of *ana* with which to act.

Ana, lest it be misunderstood as a rational bureaucratic type of power, stands in need of supernatural intervention and protection. Dictators have to be aided by intermediaries trained in esoteric arts, such as astrologers and numerologists, to anticipate threats and head off challengers. They can do this by visiting sites where confluences of supernatural power can be accessed and by participating in rituals to anticipate and outperform future unwanted events – or by forcing others to participate in them. Those others might include anyone who has ever travelled by road in Myanmar, since one well-known story goes that the reason drivers in Myanmar, then Burma, were ordered from the left to the right side in 1970 was that an astrologer advised General Ne Win that via this expedient he would avert a right-wing putsch.

Awza denotes another type of power. This type gives those in whom it accrues, through education, **race**, religion and the arrangements of **patriarchy**, opportunities to say and do things that others cannot. This is power that (like *ana*) exists as a force in the world; like two other types of *awza* with which it is lexically linked – the *awza* of nourishing food, which gives creatures life, and the *awza* of healthy soil, on which plants thrive – it is a nutrient, not an instrument. Though somebody may be possessed of *awza*, they cannot wield it. This does not mean that it is not in their service. They can influence others to do their bidding. But the power/*awza* to influence others issues from elsewhere than that of power/*ana*. The latter power is in the form of commandment exemplified as sovereign power. The former is relational. *Ana* can be obtained and moved about through mundane and supramundane interventions. *Awza* has potency that is tangible but not transferable.

There are, to be sure, other words that denote power. Among them, *bôn* (sometimes Romanised as *hpoun*), is a type of power that accrues through meritorious action. It is manifest in the form of the Buddhist monk, the *bôngyi*, or one with great *bôn* (see the entry on **Buddhism**), since having adequate power of this sort, accrued from the deeds of previous lives, is a condition of possibility to become a monk. It correlates with *awza* inasmuch as it radiates rather than dominates. Another is the English loan term *pawa*, which rocker Lay Phyu's album *Power 54* adopted back in 1996. Fifty-four is the number of Aung San Suu Kyi's house on University Avenue. The number disappeared from official labels when censors belatedly got the reference and cassettes circulated as mere *pawa*, with the 54 in their ellipses, on crooners' lips in the karaoke bars and teashops of **dictatorship**.

Perhaps the *pawa* in *Power 54* was meant to refer not to either *ana* or *awza* but to both. *Ana* and *awza*, after all, are not mutually exclusive. The power of the ideal political leader is constituted by each. Military dictators are far from ideal. They have a surfeit of *ana* and an exiguity of *awza*. Aung San Suu Kyi, by contrast, has come close to the ideal. This is why, as leader of the National League for Democracy and people's champion, she has constituted a surpassing threat to the military – one that it has been unable to contain other than by preventing **politics**. General Aung San, her father, in death achieved the ideal by virtue of his lifelong struggle for national liberation and martyrdom. His daughter carries his legacy.

While Aung San Suu Kyi's *awza* derives in no small part from her father, genealogy is but part of the story. The power of Suu Kyi's *awza* is that it is at once hereditary and cultivated, through religiously imbued practices of self-discipline, which inform her idea of **freedom**; her bilingual eloquence, which brought her to prominence at mass demonstrations in 1988; her performed selflessness; and, for over three decades, her unbroken commitment to her Burman (or *Bama*) **race** among other national races. In the 1990s she refused to leave the country, and with it the struggle for democracy, even as her husband lay dying in Oxford, lest she be denied re-entry. In 2017 she refused to criticise the Myanmar state when it stood accused of **genocide**. For people abroad, these two positions might look contradictory: the one in defence of human rights, the other in defence of their violators. At home they do not. Both were in defence of the nation. Both enhanced Suu Kyi's *awza*.

The **reform** era of the 2010s was a testing time for power not only for the military and for Aung San Suu Kyi and her party but also for others in government or dealing with government. People who were new to the experience of being in proximity with power/*ana* wanted to try it out. These include members of the legislatures at the union level and those in the seven subnational regions (Ayeyarwady or on an earlier Romanisation Irrawaddy, Bago or Pegu, Magwe or Magway, Mandalay, Sagaing, Tanintharyi or Tennasserim, Yangon or Rangoon) and seven states (Chin, Kayah or Karenni, Kayin or Karen, Kachin, Mon, Rakhine or Arakan, Shan). They included the likes of the new commissioners for human rights and corruption, the Union Election Commission, and the leaders and representatives of armed groups in ceasefire talks or deals.

Throughout this decade the military ceded a quantum of power/*ana* to civilians in these and other agencies, but it never relinquished it. As well as holding one-quarter of the seats in the union legislature (see the entry on **Politics**), it retained the ministries of defence, border affairs and home affairs, the last of which oversaw the police force, prisons and the fire brigade, which has an auxiliary security function. Its men sat at tables in tripartite ceasefire negotiations, with civilians from government, while armed groups demanded rights to **development** and debated the meaning of **federalism**. Through these processes it succeeded in winning civil war by keeping belligerents at the negotiating table and enhanced its status by being in proximity with Aung San Suu Kyi.

It should be clear from this entry that, among different types of power, *ana* clashes whereas *awza* absorbs. *Awza* has no resources with which to resist the coercive force of *ana*. But if its power is great enough, *awza* can deaden the effects of *ana*. It can render the master of that type of power, the *anashin* or dictator, politically speaking a pathetic figure whose sovereign commands ring hollow – whose achievements, if they can even be called that, remain limited to the prevention of **politics**.

3 Dictatorship

အာဏာရှင် / anashin / n dictator.
အာဏာရှင်စနစ် / anashinzanit / n dictatorship.

The content of the legislator's action is right, but devoid of legal power: it is powerless right. Dictatorship is omnipotence without law: it is lawless power. – *Carl Schmitt,* Dictatorship

Unlike the English word 'dictator', whose origins in Renaissance interpretations of a Roman republican office for dealing with emergencies Carl Schmitt traced in his 1921 book on the topic, the Burmese word *anashin* is descriptive, not juridical. The dictator is nobody other than one who masters *ana*, **power**. His is indeed a lawless **power**, but it is not freed from legal restrictions through certain arrangements to resolve an abnormal situation like a war or rebellion. Though war and rebellion have been justifications for the military's repeated usurpation of **power** in Myanmar, these are false motives; pretexts to seize power, *ana-thein*. Dictatorship in Myanmar is not a means to an end, except inasmuch as its ends are immanent. The point of dictatorship is to constitute a dictator.

In Myanmar, with the exception of the constitutional emergency government, which General Ne Win temporarily headed from 1958 to 1960 when the civilian legislature continued working under constrained circumstances, every military government that has followed has been despotic (see the entry on **Politics**). None have heeded constitutional order. Usurpers in 1962 (General Ne Win) and 1988 (General Saw Maung) never even bothered to revoke the constitutions that the military state superseded. As they had grabbed **power**/*ana* lawlessly, they had no reason to bother with powerless right.

General Ne Win, who in civilian guise later went by the handle U Ne Win (*U* being the honorific for an adult male, like 'mister' in English; *Daw* the equivalent for women) was the prototypical *anashin* who set the terms and tone for those who followed him. He was petty, his efforts parochial, his **power** adequate. The party dictatorship he established was his own, not the masses'. Burma never leapt forward into upheaval of the sort that the communist party brought to China. Ne Win's party didn't engineer a program for radical economic and cultural transformation. He didn't want it to do that, and the party couldn't have done it even if he had. The Burma Socialist Programme Party was not that type of mass organisation. Ne Win was not that type of dictator. Burma was not China.

This is not to imply that there were no major changes in Ne Win's time. In the mid-1960s the Revolutionary Council nationalised private enterprises. These included newspapers and printing presses, ending what little remained of public communications that were not those of the coming party-state. It dispossessed large landholders and non-natives (see the entry on **Race**) of capital that it concluded would be better off in its own hands or in those of native peasants whom it addressed as a core constituency. With the 1974 Constitution it integrated party and state functionaries horizontally. While keeping them formally separate, it collapsed the executive, legislature and judiciary into one another.

Throughout these decades, soldiers and police contained **politics** by putting down public protests as they arose, like those that accompanied the Southeast Asian Peninsular Games in 1969 and the workers' and students' demonstrations of 1974 and 1975. But protests in 1988 wouldn't let up. The military shot its way back to **power**, jettisoned the party state and returned its men to the foreground of government. Two more dictators followed: General Saw Maung from 1988 to 1992, whom Senior General Than Shwe pushed aside to become and remain chairman of the ruling military junta in each of its iterations (the State Law and Order Restoration Council to 1997 and then the State Peace and **Development** Council to 2011), until the beginning of the short-lived **reform** era.

After the junta back-pedalled on the 1990 election result, it took out its frustrations on what it labelled internal destructive elements. People who spoke up loudly for democracy or **federalism** or human rights disappeared into an obscure network of **interrogation** camps. Through intrusive and arbitrary administration, Saw Maung and then Than Shwe kept everyone else in check and themselves in **power**. All attempts at forcing them out, whether through use of arms or through unarmed protest, failed. In the end, it was via a staged constitutional referendum in 2008 and then an election in 2010 that dictatorship gave ground, with the establishment of new legislatures in 2011, to **politics**.

Things were changing, and lasting change began to look inevitable when the National League for Democracy won a first election in 2015 and a second one in 2020. But Myanmar's armed forces hadn't gone anywhere. They were no longer at the forefront of all national affairs, but they were far from out of the picture.

Army officers ran ministries, planned for **genocide**, talked about **federalism**, profited from economic **development**, and were visible to all and sundry as a bloc sitting in one-quarter of the national legislature. Military spokesmen sounded vociferous complaints about the conduct of the 2020 vote, and in January the next year their commander-in-chief, Senior General Min Aung Hlaing, uttered threats about the consequences of not heeding the military's concerns.

A few days later, Min Aung Hlaing usurped **power** and became the country's fourth military dictator since 1948. He broke from his predecessors by insisting that he was acting in accordance with the military's own 2008 Constitution, by abducting the civilian president and putting a former army officer in his place (see the entry on **Sovereignty**). After a brief interval, protests began. Within a few weeks, they had enveloped towns and cities up and down the country. Once the shooting started, **politics** spilled into **revolution**. The **reform** era that the army had taken over a decade to engineer was finished. With it went prospects for brokering a federal union.

4 Federalism

ˈfɛd(ə)rəlɪz(ə)m noun. 118. (The principle of) a federal system of government; advocacy of this …

In order to achieve lasting and sustainable peace, we agree to … Establish a union based on the principles of democracy and federalism in accordance with the outcomes of political dialogue and in the spirit of Panglong …
– *Nationwide Ceasefire Agreement, 2015; official translation*

The Myanmar Language Commission's Burmese–English dictionary contains no entry for federalism. Nor does the Commission's five-volume concise Burmese dictionary redress the oversight. Both contain definitions for the alphabetically adjacent English loan terms, fascism, *petsit-wada*, and fashion, *pet-shin*. But federalism, *petdarè-wada* or *petdarè-zanit*, depending on whether one is talking of federal ideology (*-wada*) or a federal system (*-zanit*), has disappeared into the dictionaries' ellipses.

It may be that the omission was unintended. Even so, the unintended can be telling. Before the 2010s federalism was rarely mentioned in Myanmar. Participants at seminars in territory occupied by armed groups representing various national races along Myanmar's borders, as well as those in training programs in the offices of exile groups in Thailand or India, talked about it. People in the country did not. It is not that they were not interested, but for the military federalism was a euphemism for separatism: a threat to the union that it could not tolerate as guardian of national **sovereignty** and territorial integrity.

Soldiers insisted that they had gotten involved in **politics** in the first place to counteract this threat. The military had to usurp **power** in 1962, their story goes, to prevent hereditary Shan rulers from pulling out of the union. The threat of secession followed an earlier proposal to amend the 1947 Constitution of Burma, which marked the end of British colonial rule, to make a federal instead of unitary government. The Shan leaders had only agreed to enter the union on condition of autonomy. A constitutional proviso granted a right of secession to any state whose representatives were unhappy with how things were going – once they had waited for at least a decade after independence. Aung San, the country's independence hero, had reached this agreement with representatives of groups in frontier areas at the town of Panglong, in southern Shan State, and it has been popularized as the Panglong Agreement.

It is to the spirit of this agreement that negotiators in the 2010s repeatedly referred, not least among them Aung San Suu Kyi, since her father was instrumental in making it a success. Panglong made postcolonial Burma a reality. In 1962 the reality changed. General Ne Win's takeover put an end to that deal and dashed hopes for a federated state. The only way that Shan or Kachin or whichever racialised minority would secure the autonomy they sought would be by fighting for **freedom**. And so they did.

Since then, much time and energy has been spent in combat among multifarious armed groups who have asserted **sovereignty** over one slice or another of Myanmar's territory. In the 1990s and 2000s, many harboured hopes that Myanmar would fragment as the former Yugoslavia had. One reason it did not was that while the State Law and Order Restoration Council that seized **power** in 1988 fought multitudinous enemies it sought terms on which to cede territory to certain armed groups through bilateral ceasefires. Not all the seventeen ceasefires its officers negotiated held. But enough of them held long enough for the military to stitch together a patchwork of relationships that meant at any given time it didn't have to fight on all fronts. Nor was it ever fighting against a united front.

With the reforms of the 2010s, things changed. Federalism was no longer a topic that the military would not or could not broach. Some people said that the 2008 Constitution, which was authored under the military's watch, could be read as conceding to a kind of federalism without saying as much. Under its terms, the fourteen state and regional legislatures can raise revenue through taxes on land, buildings, basic services and excise. They can make decisions about commerce and agriculture, electricity production, forestry and mining; manage roads, bridges, ports and transport; and oversee cultural and social affairs. However, governments of subnational states and regions lack autonomy. They are subordinated to Naypyidaw, where formal political **power** remains concentrated. So regardless of whether it can be read as allowing for a kind of half-sail federalism, like the half-sail democracy that Thailand's military has practised, Myanmar's constitution does not envisage or articulate a quasi-federal political order.

Nevertheless, in the **reform** era federalism was now an accepted topic of discussion among military representatives, their civilian counterparts in government and negotiators for armed parastates in frontier areas. Discussions were no longer one-on-one affairs. They brought a lot of different groups to the table for comprehensive negotiations from which but a handful of belligerents were excluded, chief among them the Arakan Army, which had formed in 2009, much later than most other groups. Myanmar's soldiers were prepared to entertain federalism notionally, at least – as the text of the 2015 Nationwide Ceasefire Agreement with eight armed groups shows. Whether they were at all persuaded by the idea is another story. It might be that they used it as a stalling tactic, to keep negotiators from armed groups in the room. After all, if everybody wanted to talk about federalism but had divergent ideas about what it meant, then the chances that progress could be made towards it were remote.

Consequently, despite superficially favourable conditions the decade of efforts towards this end accomplished precious little, at least at the national level. By the late 2010s Myanmar was no closer to a deal that would end fighting and transform the country into a federal union than it had been before the National League for Democracy came to government in 2016. In parts of the country there was progress on decentralisation, but the promise of federalism lay far off.

In the meantime, parastates did as much ceasefire state-making as they could. The idea was that, regardless of what was agreed, they would materially have in place, at least provisionally, institutions that they could substitute for those of the union – schools to teach local languages; courts and police forces to deal with certain categories of offences consistent with local ideas of justice; departments of land, agriculture, forestry and the environment.

When the military usurped **power** in 2021, the **reform**-era negotiations came to an abrupt end. Although the military insisted that it wanted to continue talks, fighting soon renewed in parts of the country that had been peaceable beforehand, including in Chin, Kachin, Shan, Karenni (Kayah) and Karen (Kayin) States. Certain groups, like the Kachin Independence Organization, came out in support of the new National Unity Government, which had formed in April to stand in for the National League for Democracy government that had been unable to sit. They and others gave training and lent arms to people's defence forces bubbling up all over the place: notably, in parts of Sagaing and Magway Regions where armed groups had not previously been active (see the entry on **Revolution**). The Arakan Army, which the government had classed as a terrorist group and excluded from negotiations in the 2010s, condemned the coup and remained in combat but did not extend its activities beyond its home territory in Rakhine State or publicly back the National Unity Government. Others, like the United Wa State Army and the Shan State Progress Party, refrained from commenting or acting on the changed conditions.

The National Unity Government for its part has committed to the idea of a federal system of government and a federal army. It has a minister of federal union affairs. It has revivified an earlier idea from a 2011 coalition of armed groups that had proposed a federal union army before the negotiations of the 2010s got underway. That proposal remained on paper. In May 2021 the revolutionary government established its People's Defence Force as a step towards its goal of a federated force for a federal Myanmar and an assertion of its determination to contest **sovereignty**.

5 Sovereignty

အချုပ် / agyôk / n 1 person in full charge of an undertaking. 2 Anything of the highest kind or order . . .

အချုပ်အခြာ / agyôkagya / n 1 same as အချုပ် n 1. . . .

အချုပ်အခြာအာဏာ / agyôkagya-ana / n sovereignty.

Don't be overcome with sadness if I die, for my death will have been in the struggle for popular will over national sovereignty. – *Ko Thiha Tun, undated letter, 2021*

The pretext for the army's usurpation of **power** in 2021 was, as previously, threats to the integrity of sovereignty. Unlike previously, the military claimed to act in defence of popular sovereignty, *pyithu agyôkagya-ana*, rather than old-fashioned state sovereignty, *naingngandaw agyôkagya-ana*. The electoral process had, the military said, been undermined by the National League for Democracy and the Union Election Commission. It fell to the military to restore the people's right to have their sovereign power acknowledged. The problem was that the military had no rightful basis to declare a state of emergency within the terms of the 2008 Constitution. President U Win Myint would not give that right. The military solution was to abduct the president and install one of his deputies, a former army officer, in his stead. The officer then signed an order for a state of emergency and handed **power** to the commander in chief, Senior General Min Aung Hlaing.

If the charade was intended to demonstrate a legalistic concern for the niceties of a constitutional order that the military had itself fashioned, then it failed to persuade anyone. What it succeeded in doing was underscoring the supreme contempt that Myanmar's military has for **politics** and for any part that citizens might play in them. Protesters who took to the barricades against the new **dictatorship**, like Ko Thiha Tun, a young medical doctor whom soldiers shot dead on the street in Mandalay, were explicit that they were in a fight first for survival and secondly for sovereignty. Against the military's conception of sovereign **power** as referent object of security for a preeminent security state, protesters embodied sovereignty in coming together politically. In 2021 sovereignty was contested in Myanmar when citizens enjoined one another to make claims that were not controlled by institutional terms for its demarcation. That is to say, they contested sovereign **power** and the concept of sovereignty itself.

People in Myanmar are well prepared to do this. Sovereignty has long been a recurrent topic among writers and speakers on **politics** in Burmese. Historians, commentators and agitators have all made it their business to remind everyone else of how sovereignty, *agyôkagya-ana*, was lost to the British with the fall of Mandalay in 1885, the exile to India of the last king of the Konbaung dynasty and the indignity of colonial domination. British sovereignty came through armed conquest, policed occupation, legislated violence and racialised administration. All these features of colonial rule passed over into the period after political independence from 1948: in wars fought against groups with competing claims to sovereignty going under various banners, ideological and racial; and in the policing of postcolonial citizens in the manner of colonial subjects.

When in the 1990s and 2000s Myanmar's military did its best to prevent party **politics**, it fell back on sovereign **power**. Sovereignty was something over which it could have the final say. The perpetuation of sovereignty became one of its catchphrases and a feature of its 'national' political scheme. In this scheme, sovereign **power** is inert. It has no force of its own. Sovereignty has to be cared for. It is critical to the survival of the state but vulnerable to attack. It stands to reason that sovereignty will always be in need of guardianship. This is the role that the military assigned to itself. To defend sovereign **power** against its enemies is the burden that the military has to bear – its heaviest duty. To do this it needs no external authorization. It is itself the author of this authority and the exclusive actor. The military is, in its scheme of things, the only institution capable and meritorious enough to succeed in this task of national **politics**. The premise is that, without it playing this role, sovereignty would be lost. The Union of Myanmar would cease to exist.

In this way, the military relates to the citizen not through binding obligations of care and assistance but out of benevolence or goodwill. By its own lights, this practice reaffirms the moral superiority of its leadership and the inevitability and indispensability of its guardianship role. This role contrasts with that of all party political opponents of **dictatorship**, above all the National League for Democracy, others like the Shan Nationalities [National Races] League for Democracy, which has been competitive in the country's vast northeastern state, armed groups in frontier areas who lay claims to sovereign control of subnational territories and their occupants, and myriad activists in the country and their allies abroad.

If sovereignty is for Myanmar's military a referent object of security, then the corollary is that the **citizen** is a latent security threat. The threat is realised when the likes of Ko Thiha Tun band together with others and through their words and deeds challenge the military's prevention of politics. Hence, though successive juntas have enjoined citizens to defend sovereignty, the exhortation has not been a call to action but a warning to remain inert. Politically active people like Thiha Tun endanger sovereignty and, hence, themselves. Politically inert people endanger neither.

That is not how Myanmar's citizens have seen things, not, in any case, if the size and heterogeneity of the protests against military **dictatorship** in 1974, 1988, 2007 and above all 2021 are anything to go by – 'above all' in 2021 because what it means to be a **citizen** has, through the struggle for sovereign **power** and the **revolution** that has followed from the protests of that year, been thrown into doubt. In contesting not only the sovereign **power** of the military state but the military conception of sovereignty, people like Thiha Tun have created conditions in which it might be possible to make themselves citizens as they will. The **citizen**, they have shown, is not someone who is formed at the end of political upheaval. The **citizen** is formed, rather, in upheaval, not because sovereignty has been successfully contested but because it has been plausibly disputed by people enacting citizenship and upsetting sovereign **power**. Because sovereignty has been contested, citizens in Myanmar have, in resistance and in **revolution**, refashioned themselves.

6 Citizen

နိုင်ငံသား / naingngantha / n citizen.

> Myanmar citizens are those national races and subgroups, being Kachin, Kayah, Kayin, Chin, Bama, Mon, Rakhine, Shan, etc., having permanently resided in some part of the national territory as their original country anterior to the year 1185 Myanmar Era, 1823 Christian Era. – *1982 Citizenship Law, section 3, unofficial translation*

In 1948, almost anyone residing in Burma could opt to be a citizen: a child or son, *-tha*, of the state or polity, *naingngan*. The struggle for **freedom** from British colonial subjugation had been hard fought and won. Burmese and Indian nationalists had had a common cause. People from throughout Asia for whom Burma was now home had joined the anti-colonial struggle there. Many died for it. Some of those responsible for the newly independent country's constitution and laws on citizenship and residency had a cosmopolitan and elite liberal vision of the citizen as someone who came into being by joining in a modern polity rather than by virtue of their lineage alone. They drafted laws accordingly.

After the military usurped government in 1962, the situation changed. The new Revolutionary Council declared that the country was burdened with unscrupulous foreign exploiters of honest workers. By dispossessing them of capital, **dictatorship** made life unbearable for hundreds of thousands who had lived in Burma for decades. For many, those decades were the whole of their lives. It put tens of thousands onto boats to India and to what was then East Pakistan, later Bangladesh. In 1978 the Burma Socialist Programme Party state, which followed the Council, launched a policing campaign to reclaim Burma's frontiers, or those few parts of them over which it had control, for citizens. This led to a forced exodus of Muslims to Bangladesh. Official accounts have it that most of those who fled returned under a bilateral agreement. But the agreement struck a nerve. Party chairman and dictator Ne Win had a commission set up to reexamine the question of who should be a citizen and draft a new law on the same.

Under the 1982 Citizenship Law (in Burmese the Citizen Law, *Naingngantha Ubade*), citizens are those people descended from others born in the territory today designated Myanmar anterior to 1823, the year preceding the first Anglo-Burmese war, which ended with a treaty and the occupation by the British of coastal areas and towns in the territory's west and east. To produce genealogical evidence of the sort that the law demands would be an impossible task for almost anyone in Myanmar. But the law does not demand evidence from everyone. Only those whose claims to be citizens are suspect must have their citizenship vetted. Everyone else gets waved through.

The difference between those who are suspect and everyone else has in practice come down to **race**. To be exact, it has come down to the colonial-era discursive differentiation of native and non-native – Indian, Chinese – subjects, now classed as national races and others. Military governments in the 1990s and 2000s sharpened the difference through arrangements to deny racialised others citizenship in the name of **sovereignty** (see entry on **Genocide**). At the same time the military kept the citizen in abeyance through the general prevention of **politics**. The citizen was nowhere to be found. Either they were no longer a citizen because they were racially suspect or they had had their citizenship affirmed but were warned against saying or doing anything in the manner of a citizen lest they threaten state stability.

That is how things were in Myanmar up to the late 2000s and early 2010s. Then events took a different turn. As the **reform** era began, the military conception of public order through the prevention of **politics** met with a reemergent citizenry. The reformed citizen was no longer obliged to remain inert – to be seen but not heard. Provided that their words and actions did not threaten sovereign **power**, they were entitled, up to a point, to stand up, speak out, talk back. And they did: in mass demonstrations over land confiscation; in press conferences demanding an end to military **impunity**; in calls to protect the country's rivers, mountains and forests from cronies who were draining, digging and cutting away in the name of **development**. Instead of, as previously, being a subject of **power** who had to supplicate office holders, with no expectation of reply or intervention, the reformed citizen tested office holders' **power** by making morally imbued claims upon it. They were soon someone to be reckoned with. Citizenship was something again worth fighting for.

Talk of rights in Myanmar now shifted from universal principles of human rights, which opponents of **dictatorship** had championed, to the rights of the citizen versus the non-citizen, of national **race** versus non-national **race**; **Buddhism** versus other faiths. The citizen reemerged as a duty-bound defender of the rights of the majority (Buddhist, Burman or combined national races) against the rights of this or that minority. Instead of colliding with the army's conception of sovereign **power**, citizens were now enlisted to help care for it, through violence directed against people whom belligerents denied were citizens who, apologists said, did not deserve to be: people classed as racial and religious others. The reformed citizen was egged on and let loose. Mass killing and assault of Muslims in 2012 and 2013 forced hundreds of thousands of people to flee from northern Rakhine State, in the country's west, to Bangladesh. It augured the genocidal violence of 2017, which in turn portended the atrocities that followed the 2021 military takeover.

As protests from abroad became more vociferous, the language of **sovereignty** became more bellicose. People who in the 2010s had flocked to Myanmar from Europe and North America to take up roles in projects for the rule of law, democracy and human rights were dismayed to find that citizens whom they had taken on as reliable partners or trusted intermediaries in projects for national **development** showed little or no sympathy to the plight of hundreds of thousands of Muslims not only in Rakhine State but elsewhere in the country who were forced to flee or risk being beaten, raped or murdered, their houses, villages and town wards torched. The reformed citizen, it turned out, wasn't going to be fashioned into a liberal image of rule-of-law subjectivity at all. Myanmar's racialised category of citizenship was not up for negotiation either – no matter the consequences. The more that foreign experts, international organisations and Internet commentators expressed shock and disgust at what was happening (see the entry on **Genocide**), the more Myanmar citizens dug in their heels. All parties were dismayed. Myanmar citizens had expected to be better understood. After all, weren't they the victims of yet another attempt to undermine **sovereignty** through foreign encroachment and cultural subjugation? Was it their fault that when provoked they defended themselves, their territory, their rights as citizens? Wouldn't Europeans or North Americans or anyone else do the same, in their situation?

The **revolution** that followed the military's usurpation of **power** in 2021 has changed the terms for brokerage of Myanmar citizenship and pushed these kinds of rhetorical questions to one side. Protesters who took to the streets and then barricades in 2021, who joined civil disobedience campaigns, mushrooming defence forces and other initiatives to drive the military out of government for good, have reopened the category of the citizen for negotiation. This is not to say that everyone who has resisted the military takeover has stopped being racist. Though many people have expressed belated remorse that they did not speak out against or do something about the demonisation of Rohingya and anti-Muslim sentiment when they had a chance, racism does not melt away in the heat of political struggle. But in it, the meaning of *naingngantha* is again being contested. New lines will have to be drawn between who is a citizen and who is not. In this way, Myanmar citizens might yet redeem themselves from their recent past and rescue **politics** from **race**.

7 Race

လူမျိုး / lumyo / n 1 race, nationality. 2 nation (as in တိုင်းပြည်နဲ့ ~ အတွက် [for country and ~]). 3 type (of people); character.

လူမျိုးစု / lumyozu / n ethnic group.

တိုင်းရင်းသား / taingyintha / n native of a country.

Race / **Faith** : Burman+Chinese-Burman / Buddhism
Race / **Faith** : Burman-Intha+Shan / Buddhism
Race / **Faith** : Malay+Burman / Islam – *Entries on Citizenship Scrutiny Cards, photographs posted online, 2022*

Much has been written about the **politics** of ethnicity in Myanmar, less about those of race. But in Burmese the two are inseparable. The word for race is *lumyo*. Ethnic group is *lumyozu*, where *-zu* designates a group or class. In daily usage, *lumyo* (sometimes, *amyo*) connotes race, nationality or ethnicity. Yet *lumyo* denotes nothing other than a type, *-myo*, of person, *lu*, a word that in principle might apply to, say, a person's gender or class as well as to their race.

That *lumyo* signifies race and not gender or class or some other human kind is a result of British colonial administration. During the first four decades of the twentieth century, large numbers of migrants entered Burma, in particular from neighbouring India, to which the territory was tethered by the British Empire, and from China. The new arrivals encountered others whose forebears had migrated to the region in earlier centuries, with whom they had affinities and differences.

The categories of British colonial administration were premised on a different theory of knowledge from their predecessors. They had different objectives. In earlier times the radical distinction drawn among kinds of people within lowland political communities in mainland Southeast Asia was between royalty and commoners. Other salient categories established class or caste-type relations between superiors and inferiors. These categories rank-ordered people by birth. But the conditions for membership in one category or another were not rigid. Physical attributes and demonstrated prowess meant that people could pass from lower to higher categories. The conditions for moving between categories themselves changed over time. And people could always opt to form more egalitarian political communities in upland areas beyond the easy reach of lowland polities.

British administrators, by comparison, sorted people into ostensibly nominal categories along racial lines. European administrative racism was, in the mid-to-late nineteenth century, at its apogee. It had been liberated by pseudo-scientific theories of descent that put Europeans naturally at the apex of world civilization. The racial schemes for organising colonial subjects were not explicitly rank-ordered, but effectively they were, for two reasons. First, Europeans were, by their own criteria, superior to everyone else; and secondly, the British distinguished non-native subjects from their native others.

As colonial government tinkered with schemes to turn colonial subjects into races, it correlated scientistic data that its men supposed they had uncovered from close observation of the shapes and sizes of adults' craniums or babies' birthmarks with attributes of social groups on whom its administrators reported. They mashed physiognomy and ethnology together and came up with naturalist explanations for lassitude, criminality and martial qualities. These they correlated with socially constructed and administratively reified cultural and linguistic categories. In this way the logics of race penetrated all aspects of colonial government. Subject races were brought into existence and rank ordered depending on the attributes that administrators assigned them. Race became the locus on which colonial rule turned in Burma, not because of the genius of colonial administrators for scientific discovery but because they made a racialised world on the terms that scientism provided.

The representatives of various races, thus classed, over time enacted the categories they were assigned. If the logic of colonial administration was racial then it was logical to identify racially. Race became a thing to be reckoned with. The fortunes of political and cultural elites came to rest on their racial identities. When, after 1948, the newly independent state failed to deliver on the promise of a federation in which racially and linguistically diverse people would be equals, recently racialised groups took up arms. The racist world that British colonial administration created turned into a world of racial conflict.

This conflict helped to enlarge and strengthen the state military and justify **dictatorship**. When the Revolutionary Council usurped **power** in 1962 it used the threat to **sovereignty** posed by Shan separatism as one of its pretexts. It reanimated colonial categories of native and non-native subjects, using them to identify internal enemies and defend the nation against them. The difference from earlier was that now the native or national race would be the general ideal type; the non-native or other type, a political and cultural inferior.

In doing this the Council coupled *lumyo* with another word that up to then had had little political significance in postcolonial Burma, namely *taingyintha*. Nowadays *taingyintha* translates as 'national race'. Plural, it is 'national races' or 'nationalities' – though in English it is commonly translated as 'ethnic races' or 'ethnicities', as in the English title of the Ministry of Ethnic Affairs. But *taingyintha* does not denote ethnicity. It is an analogue for the generic colonial category of the native.

As with the colonial taxonomies of native and non-native subjects, the national races schema is on paper nominal and in practice ordinal. At the top of the hierarchy, or at the centre of the array of the eight races in the schema – the seven minor ones being Kachin, Kayah (or Karenni), Kayin (or Karen), Chin, Mon, Rakhine (or Arakanese) and Shan – are the majority Burman, or *Bama*. Outside the schema come all those acknowledged non-national races, like Chinese, Bengali and Nepali.

Among non-national races, Chinese cut the most ambiguous figure. This is not only because the word for Chinese, *Tayôk*, lumps Sino-Burmese shop-keepers together with migrant workers from Yunnan, gems traders from Guangdong, executives from Beijing, tourists from Singapore and religious pilgrims from Taiwan. It is because Chinese in Myanmar are accorded a special relationship of kinship, which is conveyed by another word in Burmese, *paukpaw*. Yet, as in other parts of Southeast Asia, Chinese people living in Myanmar have long suffered attacks by those who have classed them as outsiders and threats to social and economic well-being. Xenophobic state policies in the 1960s, 1970s and 1980s taught the Sino-Burmese population to keep quiet or get out. In the 1990s, with the partial emancipation of capital (see the entry on **Development**), Sino-Burmese businesses flourished and Sino-Burmese who left the country came back. By the 2010s everybody in government wanted Chinese capital. But anti-Chinese sentiment lingered and fostered racially articulated protests against, among other things, a project to build a dam at the Ayeyawady (or Irrawaddy) River headwaters, which the Thein Sein government suspended in 2011.

If national races' attitudes to Chinese were in the 2010s **reform** era ambivalent, then towards Rohingya they were unambiguously hostile. The reasons have to do with administrative racism. The preponderance of people in Myanmar have never met any Rohingya, who are concentrated, for historical and policing reasons, in a small area of Myanmar opposite Bangladesh. They have been confined there since the State Law and Order Restoration Council started using the 1982 Citizenship Law shortly after it took **power** in 1988 to deny them standing as citizens and, relatedly, to deny the existence of Rohingya. Denial has come first through refusal to recognise the nomenclature 'Rohingya', as if the nomenclatures of any other cultural and linguistic groups in Myanmar, or anywhere else, are not themselves socially constructed – or any less politically salient for that. And denial has come, secondarily, through refusal to recognise Rohingya as *taingyintha*, on which the possibility of collective participation in the racialised polity depends. Thirdly, it has come via innuendo and analogy which suggest that not only are these not Myanmar people but that they are suspiciously unlike human beings at all (see the entry on **Genocide**).

Were members of the political community classed exclusively as members of one or another race then it would be relatively easy to sort people out. But scientistic racism does not work like that. In Myanmar, people fall into more than one category depending on parentage and grand-parentage, like the holders of Citizenship Scrutiny Cards whose photographs circulating online denote them as children of a Burman and a Chinese-Burman, of a Burman-Intha and Shan couple, or of Malay and Burman parents. Anyone who identifies or is identified as Burman might administratively be the child of unions between people designated as Burmans and those designated as belonging to other national races, and non-natives, since the entry on the card is for *lumyo* not *taingyintha*. In practice, because to be Burman is to embody a bundle of attributes, a person who is nominally part Chinese or Shan can, if they wish, perform Burmanness by practicing Theravada **Buddhism** and speaking Burmese. A Muslim who is part Burman could become a Buddhist and do the same. Concomitantly, a Buddhist who voluntarily converts to Islam or Christianity undermines their privileged status.

The **politics** of race in Myanmar, then, contain two forces, the one centripetal and the other centrifugal. The first draws people towards the exemplary Burman, the preeminent national race and ideal **citizen**. To be Burman is to be a member of the political community 'Myanmar'. Not to be Burman is not to be excluded from this community but ideally calls for membership in another national race. Not to be a member of another national race is not to be disqualified from citizenship; however, it is to be peripheral and, for many, vulnerable. The second force pushes those who identify firmly with another national race category further into that category, and the **politics** of minority rights to membership in the national racial scheme. The goal becomes to advocate for the rights of one's own national race in relation to those of others. The combined effect of these forces is to further racialise **politics** and make for the conditions in which **genocide** is possible.

8 Buddhism

ဗုဒ္ဓဘာသာ / Budda batha / n 1 Buddhism. 2 person of the Buddhist faith.

ဗုဒ္ဓသာသနာ / Budda thathana / n 1 Buddha's Sasana; teachings of Buddha.

The state acknowledges that Buddhism and the Buddha Sasana, which the majority of citizens venerate, are replete with special qualities. – *2008 Constitution of Myanmar, section 361, unofficial translation*

The rubric for this entry is Buddhism, but its subject is the **politics** of the Buddha Sasana. Buddhism is Buddha-*batha*. The suffix -*batha* denotes faith. Hence, Christianity is Christian-*batha*; Islam, Islam-*batha*; Hinduism, Hindu-*batha*; and the like. *Thathana,* or in Pali *sasana,* refers to a religious order and its teachings. This term can pertain to any established religious order: Christian-*thathana* to refer to the Christian mission, for instance, or Islam-*thathana* for the contents, institutions and instructors of Islamic education. But for many people in Myanmar, *thathana* is nothing other than the Buddha Sasana of the Theravada tradition (as distinct from the Mahayana traditions practiced in neighbouring China): the discourses of the historical Buddha, Gautama; the Dhamma (in Sanskrit, dharma), or natural law; and the lineage of practitioners, the Sangha, and their interpretive and pedagogical works. In short, it is through the Buddha Sasana that Buddhism survives and thrives. Absent the Buddha Sasana, there would be no Buddha-*batha*.

Concern to defend and preserve the Buddha Sasana has for centuries been elemental to **politics** in mainland Southeast Asia. But the object of defence and preservation and the idea of what it means to defend and preserve the Sasana, against what threats and with what means, have changed from one period to the next. Buddhist kings throughout Southeast Asia for centuries propagated the Buddha Sasana. They fought under its banner. At times they secured their rule by purging the clergy or checking its influence. Monarchy and Sangha had fluctuating interdependent **power** relations. Sometimes monarchs allied with certain monastic orders against others. At other times the Sangha's resources enlarged to a point that it threatened the ability of a king to rule. Throughout, Buddhism was, in one way or another, a force for Buddhist monarchy to reckon with.

British imperialism threatened Buddhism not because it brought with it competing creeds – or not for this reason in particular – but because its administrators had little interest in whatever the Buddha Sasana had to offer. The British occupation of Burma was for commercial and geopolitical reasons. Christian missionaries from Europe and North America who tagged along converted many people among the cultural and linguistic minorities they encountered, but they failed to impress the majority Theravada Buddhist populace. The threat that colonial rule posed, then, was not from another dogma. It was the severing of the Buddha Sasana from **sovereignty** that made it threatening. With the exile of the last Buddhist king to India in 1886, the Sangha lost its formal role in sanctifying political order and much of the income and prestige that came with it. That was not all. It lost social functions, in particular its monopoly on the teaching of literacy and numeracy to boys through monasteries ubiquitous among towns and villages in the lowlands and in parts of the highlands like areas of the Shan plateau.

Under the circumstances, it is not surprising that Buddhist monks fell in with those fighting against the colonial takeover. Monks participated in resistance to British forces even after the fall of Mandalay in 1885. They formed part of the earliest urban political opposition in the 1910s and 1920s. As antagonism to imperial **power** hardened into durable opposition to colonial rule in the 1920s and 1930s, monks joined with intellectual nationalists and with armed enemies to colonial rule in the countryside. Buddhist adherents took a greater role in defence of Buddhism, establishing organisations like the Young Men's Buddhist Association, modelled on its Christian counterpart, to promote Buddhist values among the general population and campaign against mores that its members considered alien to Buddhism.

When colonial occupation was over, efforts shifted from defence to promotion of the Buddha Sasana. In the 1950s monks remained involved in politics. Among them were those who pushed, along with lay adherents, for Buddhism to become the state religion. It briefly did, under the last civilian government led by U Nu, before General Ne Win usurped **power** in 1962. Thereafter his Revolutionary Council began to push back against the Sangha. The Burma Socialist Programme Party that the Council established had to have a monopoly on the administration and conduct of social order. It was not going to tolerate an autonomous and intrusive Buddhist clergy. It imposed rules and introduced bodies to contain the Sangha, for instance by ordering monks to register for identification documents and by establishing an official body, the State Sangha Maha Nayaka Committee, for the oversight of clerical administration and discipline.

There were limits to what the military could do. It could not stop monks from joining the massive democracy protests in 1988 that brought down the Party. The junta that followed, the State Law and Order Restoration Council, lacked any ideological agenda or novel political theory. But it could claim moral high ground by planting the Buddhist flag and presenting itself as authentic defender of the Buddha Sasana against bogus monks and blameworthy charlatans within the religious order. It backed conservative apolitical abbots and jailed agitators and schismatics. On state television broadcasts, its officers mimicked ancient royalty by prostrating themselves on sprawling rugs before senior monks. They made oversized donations with which to construct new pagodas and repair old ones (see the entry on **Development**), and they lectured public servants on how to conduct themselves virtuously.

Once more soldiers' efforts to prevent politics were only partly effective. In 2007 monks formed the backbone of anti-**dictatorship** protests that, now in the age of the Internet, became known as the Saffron **Revolution** after the colour of their robes (though in Myanmar these are commonly copper or bronze coloured). Soldiers, police and assorted thugs raided and smashed up monasteries identified as nodes for organisation and resistance, abducting alleged ringleaders for **interrogation** and imprisonment. State media again blamed 'fake' monks for inciting others and lamented the involvement of religious men in **politics**, much as their colonial predecessors had done.

After 2011, when the **reform** era came into its own, the Sangha's political activity lurched towards the defence of **sovereignty**. Monks established the association best known by the acronym Ma-Ba-Tha, for *aMyo-Batha-Thathana saungshaukye apwè*, roughly speaking the group for the protection of the **race** or nation, faith and the Sasana. The name echoes a colonial-era nationalist slogan (which had a fourth element that Ma-Ba-Tha lacked: *panya*, wisdom or education). Ma-Ba-Tha, which in English went by the label of the Patriotic Association of Myanmar, rode the waves of anti-Muslim communal violence provoked by a loose movement identifying with the numerals 969 (enumerating attributes of the Buddhist Triple Gem, the Buddha-Dhamma-Sangha), a movement that had predated the 2010s but spread with the uptake of mobile phones and Facebook in this period.

Because Buddhist monks have a special duty to assess and respond to threats to the Buddha Sasana, they find ways into **politics** through a variety of causes. On the surface of it, these sometimes appear contradictory. But there is no contradiction between monks marching against **dictatorship** in 2007 to drive soldiers out of office and marching for enforcement of the 1982 Citizenship Law in 2012 to drive alleged Muslim foreigners out of the country. The difference in each case is just a matter of interpretation. On the first, the threat was posed by an army bent on impoverishing devotees to whom the clergy must turn for its own sustenance; on the second, against another faith that, the story goes, threatens to swallow up Buddhism and, with it, the races it nurtures and on which its survival depends. The point is not that the monkhood is at one moment progressive and another conservative. Nor is it to belabour the obvious fact that the monkhood is heterogeneous in its political composition, views and goals. It is that concern with what constitutes a threat to the Buddha Sasana and how best to defend it is inconstant. The constitution of threats and responses to them are iterative but variable – historically referential, politically contingent.

The duty to defend Buddhism is anchored in discourse about dangers to Myanmar's **sovereignty**, but in principle it exceeds the country's territory. It extends to defence of Buddhism globally. Existential threats to Theravada Buddhism might exist in all the lands where this tradition is pronounced: in mainland Southeast Asia, through Thailand, Laos and Cambodia; and in South Asia, including Sri Lanka, where monks in Myanmar have long gone to link up with politically active counterparts. Buddhists to their east should be grateful, assertive defenders of the Buddha Sasana in Myanmar say, for their efforts to defend the 'western doorway' or gateway, as the country's short border with Bangladesh is known, against the Sasana's enemies. This rhetoric of threat to a mythological Buddhist golden land, visualised in the geopolitics and demographics of mainland Southeast Asia in the twenty-first century, affirms the rightfulness of Buddhism's special place as first faith among equals and justifies violence against Muslims – even, if it comes to it, genocidal violence.

9 Genocide

dʒɛnəsʌɪd noun. m20. The (attempted) deliberate and systematic extermination of an ethnic or national group.

Can there be genocidal intent on the part of a state that actively investigates, prosecutes and punishes soldiers and officers who are accused of wrong-doing? – *Aung San Suu Kyi, addressing the International Court of Justice, The Hague, 2019*

'Genocide' is a word relatively new to the world that up until recently was not much used in Burmese. The conventional neologism, *lumyodôn thatpyat-hmu*, conveys its literal meaning: killing, *thatpyat-hmu*, to wipe out, *-dôn*, a **race**, *lumyo*. This evocative usage fails to encapsulate the full range of meanings associated with the term under the Genocide Convention. Genocide in international law is not limited to killing. It includes the causing of physical or mental harm or imposing conditions on a national, racial or religious group with the intent to wholly or partially destroy it, to deliberately and systematically exterminate it.

All armies specialise in violence. Not all have opportunities to practice it routinely. The army in Myanmar does. It is habituated to exterminating, or aiming to exterminate, people and things classed as enemies. Its soldiers are not trained for combat; they are trained in it. Propaganda exhorts them to 'crush all internal and external destructive elements as the common enemy'. This is not just metaphor. Enemies have to be pulverised. They include millions living in territory over which a multiplicity of armed groups have since independence in 1948 variously fought for fragmented **sovereignty**. It is from these territories that allegations of genocide in Myanmar first came in the 1990s and 2000s, by groups documenting indiscriminate attacks on villages and their occupants that had pushed hundreds of thousands of people into Thailand and at least as many deeper into the hills or down into the lowlands of Myanmar, away from areas where they could be killed with **impunity**, their livestock slaughtered and crops burned.

But it was with the headline-grabbing attacks on Muslims in Rakhine State in 2017 that *lumyodôn thatpyat-hmu* became familiar to people in Myanmar. The campaign that drove hundreds of thousands across the border into Bangladesh, to what soon became the largest refugee camp in the world, in Cox's Bazaar, followed an earlier period of atrocious communal violence. Attacks on Muslims up and down the country in 2012 and 2013 came after inflammatory reportage of the rape and murder, allegedly by Muslims, of a young Buddhist Rakhine woman – a person who by faith, **race** and gender was a close-to-ideal **citizen** in need of patriarchal protection and, in her violation, masculine revenge. That revenge came swiftly. Though it met resistance, the outcome was never in doubt. As melees and reprisals continued, attacks on Muslims by amorphous organised mobs spread across the country with tacit or explicit support of police and local officials.

In 2017 the army, police and paramilitaries attacked Muslim villages in the northern tip of Rakhine State. Survivors who reached Bangladesh told how soldiers and paramilitary police officers threw themselves into a saturnalia of murder, arson and sexual violence following a number of assaults on border checkpoints the year before. Members of the Arakan Rohingya Salvation Army, which formed after the atrocities in 2012 and 2013, reportedly were responsible for the attacks. Though militarily insignificant, the attacks were a false motive for the scorched-earth operation to follow, which recalled genocidal campaigns in other parts of the country. But in the mountains and hills in Myanmar's north and east, the army meets with formidable, albeit outnumbered and outgunned, opponents in asymmetrical lethal combat. In the undefended townships bordering Bangladesh, however, its soldiers and paramilitaries had little to fear. There they were not fighting. They were hunting.

Buddhist monks backed the hunt. Ashin Wirathu was by then the best known internationally. He had been imprisoned during the 2000s for religious agitation (see the entry on **Buddhism**). He was among prisoners whom the Thein Sein government pardoned in 2012, early in the **reform** era. On his release Wirathu went back to demagoguery. Facebook had arrived, and he along with other Islamophobes put it to use. He got a lot more attention than he had in the past. *TIME* magazine's Asia edition in 2013 pronounced his 'the face of Buddhist terror'. But for all that, he has neither the *awza* nor *bôn* (see the entry on **Power**) of other monks who made genocide possible. One of those is Ashin Nyanissara, the abbot of the Thidagu, or Sitagu, monastery and head of the Shwegyin Nikaya, the second-largest order of monks in Myanmar. Nyanissara has been more calculated than Wirathu, though over time less dissembling, in his incitement of anti-Muslim violence and support of the military. While posing as a lover of interfaith dialogue and a compassionate humanist in meetings with everyone from Barack Obama to Pope Francis, through parable and homily at home Nyanissara has likened Muslims to rats and cockroaches and reassured army officers of the rightness of their cause. The military commander, Senior General Min Aung Hlaing, is one of his devotees.

The outpouring of people to Bangladesh in 2017 had precedents. But on the previous occasions that huge numbers had fled military and paramilitary atrocity, in 1978 and 1991–2, a military installed party **dictatorship** and a self-installed junta had answered or ignored allegations from abroad. In 2017 international opprobrium was aimed at Aung San Suu Kyi, who was then heading the semi-civilian government and whom, people abroad mistakenly assumed, could be held to the same standards that had earned her the 1991 Nobel Peace Prize for, in the words of the Nobel Committee, her non-violent struggle for democracy and human rights.

A gulf opened between narratives in Geneva or New York and those in Naypyidaw. Elected members of a legislature without Muslim representatives voiced anxieties not about military **impunity** for atrocity but about how Myanmar had been misunderstood or misrepresented abroad. While Aung San Suu Kyi remained quiet her allies could plausibly insist that she did not have the **power** to oppose the military. In 2019 their apologies wore thin when she volunteered to go to the International Court of Justice to defend Myanmar's **sovereignty** against alleged genocide. Though in taking this step she destroyed her credibility abroad, at home she was exalted for her defence of **race** and religion against their enemies. Ironically, in her defence of genocide Suu Kyi made the reasons that the military commander could not long tolerate her in **power** all the more obvious. If by the 2020 election she was politically invincible, then the only thing left for the military to do was to prevent **politics** all over again.

Meanwhile, the Court in the Hague accepted that grounds for an inquiry exist and made an interim order against Myanmar. Lawyers will for years argue about the finer points of the definition of genocide and its applicability or otherwise to what happened in Myanmar. Investigators will assess whether evidence, which a special United Nations 'mechanism' is gathering and compiling, suffices to hold the state or its individual office bearers responsible. Its remit has now extended to evidence of the **impunity** with which soldiers and paramilitaries in Myanmar have killed, tortured, raped and pillaged since the 2021 coup. Of this there is no shortage.

10 Impunity

ɪmˈpjuːnɪti noun. m16. Exemption from punishment; exemption from injury or loss as a consequence of action, security. Freq. in **with impunity**, in such a way as to be exempt(ed) from punishment or from injury or loss.

Myanmar's transition cannot succeed without an end to the impunity that permeates all levels of the justice system. – *Yanghee Lee, Special Rapporteur on Myanmar, Human Rights Council, Geneva, 2020*

'Impunity' is, like **genocide**, a word from outside the Burmese vernacular. Like 'genocide', Burmese usages for 'impunity' are translations from English. In its English–Burmese dictionary the Myanmar Language Commission defines impunity as *dangat magan-ya-gyin* – the act of going unpunished. As far as definitions go, this is not bad, though it is ugly – the type of verbiage that lawyers swallow and regurgitate but that sensible folk shun or ignore.

This is not to imply that people in Myanmar don't care or know about impunity. They do. They just don't talk about it that way. The nationwide protests opposing the military's **power** grab in 2021 were a resounding statement against impunity. The contempt directed towards the country's latest dictator, Senior General Min Aung Hlaing, evinces a hatred of his presumption that he can do what he likes and suffer no consequences. The formation of armed local and people's defence forces to fight back was from the beginning intended to send a message to those who think they can kill with impunity: that they ought to know that they themselves can be killed.

Among youth activists at the forefront of the anti-**dictatorship** protests in 2021, the insistence that theirs be the last generation to confront the evils of **dictatorship** resonates with the anti-impunity idea in international law and its institutions. The idea's premise is that to hold soldiers responsible for alleged **genocide** or other atrocities requires a political transition. To transition is to move from one (undesirable) condition to another (desirable) one. It is to cross over from one place to the next. Impunity, in this way of thinking, is a thing of the past; accountability, the way of the future.

Myanmar's putative transition in the 2010s did not bring it any closer to an end to impunity because the conditions did not exist for this possibility. Newly elected members of national and subnational legislatures included many former political prisoners and ex-combatants for para-state armies fighting for autonomy and **federalism**. Yet the National League for Democracy brought with it no scheme for accountability for past injustices. This was not an oversight. The League actively discouraged talk of such schemes. It warned anyone who spoke of transitional justice that they misapprehended the transition that they were in. The **reform** era was not one in which people should expect accountability. Aung San Suu Kyi herself dismissed efforts to lay foundations for a reckoning with history, suggesting that they could undermine **development**.

Consequently, despite calls from people like the United Nations Special Rapporteur on human rights in Myanmar, there was in the 2010s no sustained or coordinated attempt to reckon with the violence that accompanied decades of military rule, let alone any efforts to memorialise it. The opposite happened. If **reform** meant fixing things up, then the past had to be effaced. And it was. Construction workers converted the torture chambers of a police **interrogation** centre into luxury suites for the five-star Rosewood Hotel. Gardeners manicured new shrubs on the embankments of the Inya Lake that were mute to the deaths of hundreds of student protesters, whom soldiers and paramilitary cops beat and drowned there in 1988. German experts helped to renovate the Government Technical Institute, where soldiers, cops and thugs brought and detained scores of protesters in 2007. No evidence remains of those conditions in which detainees had been kept, without washrooms or toilets, being bashed and kicked. They and countless others abducted, tortured, murdered, raped and disappeared over decades of **dictatorship** were but vague outlines on the backdrop of a new political stage upon which stood only promises of a better future.

After the 2021 coup, the military in Myanmar affirmed through its actions that there would be no reckoning with any past atrocities. Paramilitary cops and soldiers dragged dead bodies of anti-dictatorship protesters around the streets like bags of garbage. They burst into people's lives day and night, smashing vehicles and doors to abduct purported ringleaders of rallies, vociferous Facebook users and members of new urban revolutionary groups. They raided hospitals and schools, destroyed the offices of charities and killed the residents of apartments. They drove the occupants of towns where they encountered resistance into the countryside and burned their houses down. When they met with armed combatants in rural areas they ceased travelling over land and began descending on towns and villages from air to do the same (see entry on **Revolution**).

All this might give the impression that soldiers and paramilitary cops in Myanmar can get away with absolutely anything. In fact, none of it prevents certain offenders from being made accountable. Someone can always be held responsible for something. However, the punishment of a few can work to exempt the many. Far from being a check on impunity, punishment can make it durable. This was the way of things in Myanmar even before the 2010s. When in the 1990s and 2000s the former military spymaster Lieutenant General Khin

Nyunt recited statistics on numbers of personnel convicted in military or police tribunals for offences that included rape and assault, he was not making them up. All he was doing, in effect, was pointing out that selective investigations and punishments are compatible with conditions for pervasive, lasting impunity.

Khin Nyunt might also have wanted to remind his audiences that, inasmuch as all states make monopoly claims on violence, exemptions from punishment for those who are duty-bound to specialize in violence – soldiers, cops, paramilitaries, their proxies – are immanent to the state idea. Sometimes it might be necessary to make an example of somebody; at other times, not. The important thing is that those with **power** retain the prerogative to decide which offences are investigated and tried, how and when. The question of who decides, not what is decided, is politically paramount.

11 Interrogation

စစ် / sit / v . . . 2 inspect; examine; interrogate.
စစ်ကြော / sitkyaw / v Same as စစ် v 2.

I was interrogated [in 2007] for ten to fifteen days. They took about a week to break me. They got harsher around the eighth or ninth day. When they had what they needed for a case against us, they put me in the cells overnight, then sent me to Shwepyitha police station. – *Former political prisoner recounting interrogation, 2019*

This entry is the most difficult one in the lexicon, not because the term *sitkyawye*, or interrogation, is untranslatable but because it defies attempts to grasp its full significance. Like all practices associated with the captivity and torture of people, *sitkyawye* falsifies what it represents. *Sitkyawye* has an instrumental ring to it, as if interrogation were merely an instrument of **dictatorship**. It is much more than that. *Sitkyawye* reappears every time that Myanmar's soldiers usurp **power** because it is the acme of military rule.

For all the books and articles written on Myanmar's **politics**, none have conveyed the political significance of interrogation. There are biographical accounts of *sitkyawye* by those who have survived it, as well as publications on torture and extrajudicial killing as human rights problems. These list interrogation sites, *sitkyawye sagan*, past and present in military camps and police stations. They attempt to delineate and document interrogation, attending to its built environment, its personnel, their methods and the numbers of victims.

Databases, survivors' narratives and listing exercises are all important tasks in the struggle against **impunity**. Yet *sitkyawye* exceeds the sum of their parts.

It can even be obscured by them, through the impression that this institution can be confined to specific places, personnel and techniques. It cannot be, not because those methods of documentation are inadequate for their specific tasks but because those tasks do not capture its character. *Sitkyawye* is not made of bricks and mortar, zinc roofing and wire fencing. It is not made up of its interrogators, their equipment or the hours they keep. It is not its material presences or geographical extent but in its mimicry of the ideal military state, one in which a complaisant body politic is unthreatening to **sovereignty**, that *sitkyawye* comes into its own.

Sitkyawye is never publicly authorised or ordered; nevertheless, it is publicly present. Temporally, it is present every time that men who decline to identify themselves appear to take people from their houses or off the streets without explanation. Physically, it is present in a shifting archipelago of sites and practices for the arbitrary abduction, incommunicado detention and systematic torture of military targets – 'systematic' because if military rule in Myanmar has any system at all then this is it: a system to prevent **politics**, a system that in every respect aims to counter **revolution**.

Sitkyawye passes from the trays of army trucks into police lock-ups, from prisons to military bases, from rice fields to Buddhist temples. It repurposes and reconfigures what it finds. This is why specific sites for captivity and torture in Myanmar come and go with the ebb and flow of national **politics**. Arbitrary detention and torture never stopped in Myanmar during the **reform** era of the 2010s, but with political detention in abeyance and people's attention elsewhere, nobody paid much heed to occasional reports of ordinary criminal accused getting their genitals burned with cigarettes or electrocuted and pummelled to confess. Political captives, for whom *sitkyawye* as a category of practice, an institution of **power**, exists, were few. And there were other priorities like **development** and **federalism**.

Sitkyawye resurfaced the moment that the 2021 military takeover occurred. Within a month or two, stories started filtering out of protesters and political activists who had been tortured in custody. Families received the mutilated bodies of children, spouses and parents. A new *sagan* opened in a row of buildings inside an army compound at Shwepyitha, northern Yangon, to which police and soldiers took captives. One at Aungthapyay, closer to downtown, might have carried on working as it had in the 2000s. It might never have stopped working, since even at its busiest it sits unobserved in plain sight, a short distance from a shopping junction on the way to the airport, a small sign next to a boom gate instructing arrivals to report to security. Another at the old racetrack has moved elsewhere, leaving no trace. The site it occupied in 2007 has since been used by the sports ministry to house and train aspiring athletes (see the entry on **Impunity**).

In the countryside, military interrogators occupying the compounds of monasteries, schools and administrative offices after the 2021 coup transformed them into interrogation centres by restraining, beating, stabbing, suffocating, amputating, shooting and terrorising people in them whom they accused of being members or supporters of the people's defence forces that organised and armed in response to killings of unarmed demonstrators. Though army interrogators in these structure their activities in terms of information gathering, their function is to empty opponents of military **dictatorship** of their political contents and restore normal conditions of national political order. Their actions summon *sitkyawye* into existence and, with it, realise the military state in its purest form.

To reiterate, interrogation, *sitkyawye*, is not an instrument of the military state. It is the military state – or rather, it is its distillation. It is not instrumental. It is not a means to various ends, though that is how it is made to appear. It is the ends. It is not what the military state produces. It produces the military state. To destroy the military state, to cut it out by its roots, citizens will have to locate and eviscerate this behemoth. **Reform** is not adequate for this task. **Revolution** might be.

12 Revolution

တော်လှန် / tawhlan / v rebel; revolt; resist.

တော်လှန်ရေး / tawhlanye / n 1 revolution. 2 resistance.

အရေး / aye / n 1 writing; composition. 2 affair; business; matter.

အရေးတော်ပုံ / ayedawbôn / n 1 [arch] historical account of a royal campaign … 2 social or political uprising; revolution.

#အရေးတော်ပုံအောင်ရမည် / Victory to the Revolution! – *Trending hashtag on TikTok, December 2022*

Two words denote revolution in Burmese. The official encyclopedia has an entry for *tawhlanye*, which it treats as an analogue for 'revolution' in English. In contemporary usage it stands for any type of movement that pushes from an old era into a new one. It is not limited to political revolutions but includes, for instance, the Renaissance, the industrial revolution and Chinese Cultural Revolution. It is in this sense that the nomenclature of General Ne Win's Revolutionary Council, the *Tawhlanye Kaungzi*, can be understood. It was not politically revolutionary, but it registered an intention to lift the nation out of its postcolonial malaise and thrust it into a new era of socialist prosperity.

The second usage is the one in the TikTok hashtag. Here **politics** are always at stake. In its narrowest literal sense, *ayedawbôn* denotes a campaign for the seizure of sovereign **power** through uprising, rebellion and war. In its wider sense, it invokes a gamut of strategies and struggles for human **freedom**. Occupy Wall Street and general strikes that have as their objective the transformation of political economic order, like one in British Burma during 1938, can all be classed as revolutionary in this latter sense.

Both usages have had currency since the military usurped **power** in February 2021. Within a month, calls in Myanmar for the release of Aung San Suu Kyi, members of her party and others whom the military had abducted and held captive swelled and spilled out as demands for **dictatorship** to be cut at the roots and destroyed for good. As the numbers of dead grew – on streets filled with demonstrators, in apartments raided by cops and soldiers, during **interrogation** of captives – people fought back. Protesters who remained reaffirmed their positions, built higher barricades and hardened their shields. When by the end of March it became clear that these were insufficient, a new and hitherto unprecedented armed uprising began. Thousands of youths took to the countryside to seek training and arms from established para-states in frontier areas who have for decades insisted, with greater or lesser success, that military dictates stop where their territories begin. They were joined and trained by numbers of defectors from the military. Many returned to form cells in urban areas and participate in the making of hundreds of new and loosely affiliated local and people's defence forces.

From the outset the emphasis was on the need to arm for self-protection. Resisters to military dictatorship were not claiming a right to bear arms. Nor were they opting for violence because of a preference for it. Quite the opposite: theirs was violence as a last resort. Theirs was a fight for survival – and a fight for **freedom** from military enslavement, *sitkyun-bawa*. They renamed the State Administrative Council a Terrorist Military Junta. This appellation put all those embarking on armed violence against the Council not in the category of terrorists, where it would have them, but counter-terrorists. And they fought back.

So did people in Sagaing Region, which in the wake of the uprising saw an effervescence of autonomous self-defence forces, in townships like Kalay, Katha, Shwebo, Tamu, Taze and Yinmarbin, as well as Sagaing town. Many of these groups consolidated and continued to fight in loose alliances with one another after their counterparts elsewhere could not sustain their operations. They have fought absent of any overarching command-and-control structure, holding fast to the principles of defence – of themselves, their families, their towns and villages—with which they began. Although poorly armed, these and other self-defence groups have effectively forced the military state off the ground where they are operating. In such territories, troops from the Terrorist Military Junta fly in to destroy buildings and kill people, then fly out again.

This is a different situation from any in the decades before it. None of the workers' and students' demonstrations in 1974, the uprising in 1988 that gave birth to the National League for Democracy, the sporadic disturbances in the mid 1990s and the protests during 2007 in which Buddhist monks played a frontal role tipped into self-defensive armed revolution. Though after 1988 students who fled to frontier regions in the country's north and east formed the All Burma Students Democratic Front, they never stimulated widespread armed resistance of the sort that followed the 2021 uprising. And while 2007 was dubbed the Saffron Revolution, the term tethered Myanmar to a loose chain of 'colour revolutions' in Eastern Europe and other parts of the world that had preceded it, with which it had no prior relationship and little in common.

The 2021 uprising has, by contrast, produced a revolutionary situation, one in which there are plausible competing, exclusive claims to sovereign **power**, in which state authority comes under severe assault but doesn't collapse. The National Unity Government has been an important element in this situation. Though there is a risk of overstating its importance, it is an instructive case study in revolutionary planning and action when compared to its predecessor of the 1990s and 2000s, the National Coalition Government of the Union of Burma. The Coalition Government formed after the State Law and Order Restoration Council, which had usurped **power** in 1988, denied that the results of the 1990 general election, called by the junta itself, gave the National League for Democracy a mandate to govern. The Coalition Government throughout the 1990s and 2000s conducted diplomatic work of ultimately little significance, leaving military affairs to those armed para-states with which it had relations. It cooperated with groups like the exiled Burma Lawyers' Council, which set to work on one or more draft constitutions for a future federation (see the entry on **Federalism**) but didn't coordinate activities. In short, it did not act as if it were in government.

The National Unity Government, by contrast, has. It uses the existing state seal and issues notifications in the manner of government. Its ministries map onto those of the state. It has supported the setting up of civil administration and courts, reopened schools and attempted to contribute to social welfare in areas of the country where emergent armed resistance to military **dictatorship** is strongest, in particular Sagaing, and in Magway Region and Chin State. It has blocked the usurper military from taking the country's seat at the United Nations

General Assembly and set up diplomatic missions in a number of countries with tacit recognition from their hosts. It has a defence ministry and has established its own armed People's Defence Force, under which it is struggling to draw the multitudinous groups that formed after the military takeover into a command structure that many of them are unlikely to accept. Be that as it may, it has not left the war to them. It has itself declared a defensive war. It has sought to fund the war by, among other things, setting up an official cryptocurrency, issuing government bonds, and selling shares to land and buildings that the military commander Senior General Min Aung Hlaing has reportedly seized for his own use. It and its affiliates run lotteries to raise funds. Undoubtedly, the tens of millions of US dollars they have garnered through these activities amount to small change compared to the funds their adversaries have available through sale of natural gas, timber, gemstones and other commodities. However, the revolutionary Government is acting as if it is government and raising revenue to rule through routes that are recognisably those of a plausible contender for **sovereignty**. In this way it has prolonged the country's revolutionary situation.

The National Unity Government has suffered criticism for declaring a defensive war. This is, after all, not the non-violent way that Aung San Suu Kyi and earlier generations of political dissidents sought. But why should it be? The reasons for criticism are varied, but they tend to miss, or avoid, an important albeit obvious political point: the repressive violence of military **dictatorship** in Myanmar and the revolutionary violence that opposes it are not in the same category. To make this obvious point is not to apologise for specific acts of violence in the name of revolution – the shooting of alleged civilian informers or collaborators, for instance. But to equate the practice of killing informers by revolutionary forces with the killing of anti-**dictatorship** demonstrators by soldiers is to ignore the relation of the two to **power**. It is a category error that comes from treating all violence as alike by virtue of its instruments and instrumentalities.

Defensive revolutionary violence aims at the downfall of an existing order and imagines a different type of political future – one in which people might not be governed as they have been and 'the people' might be rehabilitated as a political category. It is unlike the repressive violence to which it stands opposed, not because it is itself political but because it works towards the possibility of a future that is – not a future of political **reform**, in which the military lies dormant until soldiers again make it their business to intervene, but one in which the military's capacity to intervene is destroyed. Defensive revolutionary violence, then, does not occupy the same class of practices as repressive military violence. There is in it, as collective action, a notion of **freedom** that differentiates it from repressive military violence in the name of **sovereignty**. Decades of state violence in Myanmar have produced the conditions that make revolutionary violence possible. That violence is itself premised on imagined conditions of possibility for **politics**. Defensive revolutionary violence makes those conditions imaginable. Counter-revolutionary violence promises nothing other than more of the same.

Revolutionary violence can descend into generalized, arbitrary violence absent of qualities that distinguish revolutionary action from its counter-revolutionary other. History is littered with revolutions that have gone this way. The fear of this happening in Myanmar leads people who oppose **dictatorship** to reject violence and insist on the possibility of non-violent political and social change. Those who have opted for defensive warfare counter that Myanmar's military had a decade in which to demonstrate its commitment to this possibility, and instead it showed that it will never concede to political change of the sort that the country needs. Nor have non-violent uprisings, like the one in February and March 2021, succeeded on their own terms. For revolution to succeed, they retort, violence is necessary. **Reform** is now out of the question.

13 Reform

ပြုပြင် / pyubyin / v. 1 improve; reform; rectify; set right; amend. 2 repair.

ပြောင်းလဲ / pyaunglè / v. change; transform.

Since taking up office less than six months ago, President Thein Sein has moved quickly to begin implementing his ambitious reform agenda.
– *International Crisis Group, Asia Briefing No. 127, 2011*

The watchword of government in Myanmar during the 2010s was 'reform'. This was never going to be a period of revolutionary change of the sort that General Ne Win announced when he usurped government half a century earlier, let alone violent **revolution** of the sort that followed the 2021 military takeover. As a verb, 'reform' refers to fixing up something that has fallen into disrepair, *pyubyin*, and effecting change, *-byaunglè* (*pyaunglè* where not suffixed to a Roman script vowel or *n-*). Coupled together and suffixed with *–hmu* to form an abstract noun, these two words direct the addressee's gaze forwards and backwards, towards a planned and guided better future, while recollecting a glorious past, to which it is impossible to return, yet one that might stand as a model for how things could be.

The president from 2011 to 2016, Thein Sein, was a paradigmatic reformer. As prime minister of the preceding junta that rolled its officers, him included, over into legislative assemblies and constitutional offices, his accession to the presidency met with scepticism. So Thein Sein worked hard to promote a reformist agenda, talking up clean government, accountability and transparency. But talk alone would not get him reformist credentials. After all, he had talked about the rule of law, anti-corruption measures and the like back when in uniform. If it had sounded like bullshit then, that is because it was. How to make it sound differently now that he was in civvies?

To earn reformist credentials, Thein Sein recruited specialists from abroad to advise him on how to reform everything from taxation to telecommunications, from company law to riot policing. He appointed returnee Myanmar citizens and others who had stayed at home, who had long viewed themselves as a nascent technocratic class, to positions of responsibility that they had craved but that, up until then, the military had denied them. They helped his government with its strategies to commodify land by providing tenure security for lowland small-holders while opening everything else to capital in the name of **development**.

The government launched a plan to tell a new story about an old problem: corruption. As stories go, this one is about as old as they get. The British colonisers blamed endemic corruption on the inadequacies and immorality of native subordinates. After independence in 1948, Burma's first premier, U Nu, declared it his goal to eradicate termites eating away at the foundations of government. Against the odds, his administration made some progress towards this goal. Military dictators that followed, and their subordinates, made a habit of admonishing civil servants for their waywardness and making examples out of a few to warn others against especially flagrant forms of graft or favouritism. Reformist governments of the 2010s, like their predecessors, sought to target corruption and to name and prosecute corrupt officials. Unlike their predecessors, they now had staff from a multitude of international organisations on hand with tools and indices to measure corruption's size and graphically represent its shape, to define and criminalise it. With their assistance, in 2013 the national legislature passed a new anti-corruption law. The following year the government set up an anti-corruption commission.

For a while commentators derided the commission as a paper tiger. In 2018, in a sign that it wanted the anti-corruption reform agenda to be taken seriously, the legislature pushed through an amendment to the law to empower the commission to investigate and bring cases on its own. The commission used this **power** to charge senior officials in the bureaucracy, courts and public prosecution. On some accounts, the buying and selling of outcomes in administrative matters and judicial affairs diminished or at least became less blatant; the routine gift-giving, less obvious. The military, of course, remained outside the commission's purview; the partiality of soldiers, then and since, beyond the reproach of anyone other than those in their own ranks (see entry on **Impunity**).

Meanwhile, partly owing to rivalry between Thein Sein and another former army officer, Thura Shwe Mann, who had wanted the presidency and got a house speaker's role as a consolation prize, the union legislature had turned out to be livelier and at times more combative than many commentators in the country and abroad had expected. This buoyed hopes about the prospects of Myanmar's putative transition. Experts jostled for seats on flights to its once sleepy international airports, and cars queued to hurry them along to seminars and workshops in which they talked up reform and heard what they wanted to hear. Liberal statebuilders were in desperate need of success stories, and Myanmar had the trappings of one in the making. The transition was not without challenges, but the reform agenda was still on track. If things could change for the better in Myanmar, then they could anywhere. The end of history might be nigh, after all.

On the news stands and in teashops, topics like **federalism**, democracy and human rights were no longer omitted from print and speech. Citizens found that they now enjoyed **freedom** to speak and act in ways that they could not only a few years earlier. Print media were no longer subjected to the tyranny of the censor's pencil. Almost overnight, Facebook became ubiquitous. Before the coronavirus pandemic took hold, people gathered daily on every conceivable issue. Factory workers went on strike for better wages. Buddhist monks rallied in defence of **race** and religion (see the entries on **Buddhism** and **Genocide**). Bookshops sold publications that made cases for armed groups' positions on ceasefire negotiations and regaled readers with the groups' heroic efforts for their peoples' **freedom**.

Looming large above other affairs was the question of land reform. Back in the 1960s and 1970s the Revolutionary Council and its Burma Socialist Programme Party had attacked landlordism and nationalised agricultural land and industrial sites. Agricultural cooperatives and government ministries had managed all aspects of crop production. Fixed-price procurement quotas controlled the supply of rice and other crops. The right to cultivate was tied to productivity and to a farmer's capacity to contribute to the socialist economy. After the Party state collapsed in 1988, the military kept dispossessing farmers of land, now in the name of all-round **development**. The resurgent military for a couple of decades grabbed land willy-nilly. Once reforms got going, peasants wanted it back. They and urban allies among mushrooming civil society groups organised nationwide protests that the news media reported in detail. The legislature set up an inquiry commission into land grabbing. In 2014 the commission issued a report on hundreds of cases, the majority involving the military. The report highlighted the scale of the problem but did not open avenues for redress. In 2017 the military claimed it had returned a quarter-million acres to aggrieved land holders. The claim went unverified.

Aung San Suu Kyi became state counsellor – a supra-constitutional role invented for her – and de facto president in 2016. Unlike Thein Sein, she had no need for bevies of technocrats with which to show off her reformist credentials. She herself represented reform. She embodied it. When she instead of an army officer stood at a podium to address assembled crowds or attend state ceremonies abroad on behalf of Myanmar, her presence was proof enough of change. It was in matters of **development** that she had to work hard to persuade everyone that her government was making progress. And she did. Her government picked up where its predecessor had left off. It made things in Myanmar convenient for global capital via new investment laws and policies encouraging competition for access to land. These added pressure to smallholders in parts of the country where capitalists sought to locate or expand their businesses – places like Sagaing and Magway Regions.

Reform sometimes comes across as a natural companion of progress; however, there is nothing natural about their companionship. Progress, in Burmese, is about increasing abundance. **Development** is less about the repair or renovation of anything than it is about increasing the number of things. Reform is lean. It delimits what is possible and tempers aspirations. To be developed in the sense of *punbyo* is to be enlarged. Progress is fatty. How to be lean and fatty at the same time? This was the political economic contradiction that the National League for Democracy was trying to resolve when it won a second term in office at the 2020 election. It was still trying to work it out when Senior General Min Aung Hlaing usurped **power** the following February.

By putting Aung San Suu Kyi and her party leadership back in captivity, along with many erstwhile technocrats, the military resolved the contradiction. With the political and social conditions of the reform era now in the rubbish bin, what remained for it to deal with were strictly questions of **development**. For these, **politics** would be unnecessary.

14 Development

ဖွံ့ဖြိုး / punbyo / adj prosperous; developed.

တိုးတက် / todet / adj improve; progress; advance.

As a latecomer to the development scene, Rakhine stands poised to reap the advantages of astute latecomers: learning from the success stories as well as the mistakes of those who went ahead, offering fresh openings and new horizons. – *Aung San Suu Kyi, Rakhine State Investment Fair, 2019*

Inasmuch as the military junta that, in two iterations, governed Myanmar from 1988 to 2011 was against **politics**, it was for national development. The Burma Socialist Programme Party state that had come before it was taken up with building a nominally socialist economic system. The State Law and Order Restoration Council, by comparison, just wanted to build. It wanted the trappings of a developmental regime, like its East Asian neighbours, freed from the pedantic ideology of its predecessor. In 1997 it even refashioned itself in development's image, as the State Peace and Development – *Punbyo-ye* – Council. It set up a mass association that it later transformed into the Union Solidarity and Development Party, for the purposes of filling seats in the first **reform**-era legislature from 2011 to 2015.

In slogans the military coupled *todet* with its *punbyo* to inspire a vision of technological progress up and away from the moribund industries of the socialist economic system towards a post-socialist utopia bristling with high-rises and encircled by elevated roads. Think Singapore. But what the military vision lacked that Singapore had, in its own inimitable way, was concern for the cultivation and promotion of human excellence. The Myanmar military's vision of progress was absent of people. It was obsessed with development's material form.

Development meant embracing what the Party state had once half-heartedly suppressed. If back in the 1980s the problem for the Burma Socialist Programme Party had been that the black market debilitated its socialist economic system, then the solution for the developmental military state in the 1990s was to transform the black market into the economy. All the junta had to do was to partly emancipate capital, to offer it a certain amount of **freedom** from the strictures of the earlier economic regime by liberating capitalists from constraints that had prevented them from legally obtaining significant returns on their capital. To this end, it licensed an emerging class of connected entrepreneurs to embark on projects in agriculture, mining, industry and trade.

The connected entrepreneur – in Burmese the *karoni*, from English 'crony' – became the unlikely hero of development. Among the biggest cronies were Teza, owner of the Htoo Group, which included sawmills, mining, building, hotels and Air Bagan among many environmentally destructive interests; Zaw Zaw of the Max Myanmar Group, with hotels, cement, petroleum, rubber, banking and football to his name; U Khin Shwe, a builder of many things and notorious land grabber who was one of those sitting in the 2011–15 legislature for the Union Solidarity and Development Party; and Serge Pun, a property speculator, housing developer, deforester and avid self-promoter in the Asia business media who came back to Myanmar from abroad once the army announced that socialism was a thing of the past. These and lesser cronies traded their connections with developing capital from nearby countries – China, Thailand, Malaysia – and developed capital from Singapore, Korea and Japan.

In exchange for their success, the military insisted that cronies share responsibility for the welfare of citizens by redistributing a proportion of what they made where capital did its work. Development, in contrast to the socialist economic system, signalled the withdrawal of the state from provision of threadbare public goods and minimal services – the offloading of responsibility for public welfare onto emancipated capital. In lieu of the state, tens of thousands of local welfare associations, many built from religious institutions – Buddhist, Christian, Islamic – offered assistance and provided charity to the indigent. Lawyers and doctors and dentists and drivers and people in countless other occupations across the country served needy clients at-cost or free of charge. In emergencies, these people and local civic groups surged into action. The ingenuity and resourcefulness of these groups stood out after Cyclone Nargis, the massive storm that hit the delta in 2008 killing at least 50,000 people. While soldiers stalled international rescue agencies trying to get access to the region, local groups from all over the country drove convoys of food, water, clothing and medicines to storm survivors. It was out of this experience that many prominent activists of the **reform** era formed networks, obtained skills and accrued knowledge.

None of this is to say that the state stopped being involved. But the character of its involvement changed. Soldiers, having said that they were duty-bound to get things built for the nation, needed photographic evidence that they had done this. While state agencies constructed bridges and weirs, the junta contracted cronies and coerced others into assembling or reassembling as many structures in as many places as possible: schools, hospitals, dormitories, roads – anything that could be officially opened and go into the inventory of hastily erected things. Though trained teachers were in short supply, hospitals lacked medicines, dormitories had no running water or electricity, and new roads soon rutted, so long as bricks and mortar could be observed, documented and enumerated the evidence of development was there to be had.

Bigger was better. Suspension bridges and hydropower dams, about which youthful women in costumes of various national races sang on television broadcasts, were the biggest and the best. Development was gendered: men created, women celebrated (see the entry on **Patriarchy**). Concrete erections were proof that the development dream was hardening into reality. From this fecund dream a new developed **citizen** would naturally issue, ready to cooperate in the era of **reform**. And what better place for the new **citizen** to be born than a new high-modernist capital city? In the 2000s, emancipated economic capital took about four years to complete the basic building blocks for Naypyidaw, amid hilly scrubland near Pyinmana, in the country's geographic centre. Thousands of labourers constructed the ostentatious edifices of a new legislative complex in which to contain party **politics**, alongside utilitarian buildings for government ministries and other state agencies, as well as apartments, hotels and shopping precincts to welcome the first reluctant arrivals from the Yangon-based civil service in 2006.

In the country's frontiers, development called for partnerships with armed groups whom the military sought to co-opt by granting concessions in exchange for ceasefires. The particulars of the deals differed, but in each questions about **sovereignty** or **federalism** were sidelined to keep national **politics** free from harm. Development was the only idiom in which the military would speak. These agreements brought a type of peace but not any type that ended military violence with **impunity**. To the contrary, in border areas development was predicated on use of arms and capital to resolve disputes.

During the 2010s, as sanctions regimes weakened or fell away, developed capital rushed to Myanmar from Europe and North America. Indications of development were suddenly all over the place. Apartments sprung up in which to house the refrigerators and washing machines of an emerging middle class. Better-quality roads appeared quickly. Electricity supply increased. Business consultants arrived and charged for hype and puffery. Naypyidaw stepped out from behind the bushes and onto the international stage by hosting international agribusiness summits and the World Economic Forum. Government pushed for the establishment of special economic zones and ports so as to announce to the world that development was indeed a word with which Myanmar should be associated, along with its neighbours. Environmental groups expressed concerns about the conse-quences of all this for watersheds and biodiversity, not to mention climate change. Government paid little heed. Meanwhile, life in many parts of the country continued as before but now with mobile phones and Facebook announcing that time was on the move and that, as promised, there was more of everything than ever.

Capital marched across the over two-thousand-kilometre-long border that China shares with Myanmar, materialising in new factories and roads, train and pipe lines, ports, mines and dams, and moneylending for more of the same. The Kuomintang army had once criss-crossed this border while fighting and then fleeing its communist foes, as did revolutionary commun-ists bent on the overthrow of the government in Burma. Latterly it has been the site for movements of vast quantities of goods and people, licit and illicit, weaving their way around and through the territories of armed groups like the Kachin Independence Army in northern Kachin State and the Ta'ang National Liberation Army in northern Shan State.

Noticing all this capital moving about, these armed groups and others on the border of Thailand, like the Karen National Union and its armed wing, wanted their share. In the **reform** era, development remained firmly on negotiators' agendas for ceasefire and peace talks, now complemented by substantive political questions about issues like **federalism**. The spokespeople of political parties claiming to represent national **race** groups and subnational states complained that the areas they call home had had valuable minerals, trees and gems taken from them for decades without getting anything in return. For capitalists with an eye on Myanmar, the late arrival of these states on the development scene – as Aung San Suu Kyi characterised Rakhine State – was supposed to be an opportunity for people in those states and those who represented them to see if they could not turn battlefields and massacre sites into solid ground for extractive industries.

These were happy days for development. Then things changed. Soon came allegations of **genocide**. The **reform** era lost its shine. East Asian capitalists kept coming, but Europeans and Americans started cancelling visits. The coronavirus followed. It had no recent comparators, in Myanmar or elsewhere. Though people in Myanmar have had much experience with endemic diseases, like malaria, dengue fever and tuberculosis, the country's hospitals and public health arrangements were ill prepared for this virus. It was no longer easy to keep people in Myanmar isolated from the disease, as it had been as recently as during the SARS outbreak in 2003. The country was now connected to the world economy, travel and communications in a way that it had never been before. Many more people from Myanmar were working in the capillaries of service and manufacturing industries abroad than a decade prior. The virus killed off or endangered their jobs. A lot returned home, and some brought the virus with them.

On top of all this came a constrained general election campaign in 2020 that favoured the National League for Democracy, since other parties could not get on the streets to be seen and heard. The party had another resounding victory, and with it came the promise of a third post-**dictatorship** legislature. Few people supposed that army officers would be stupid enough to again usurp **power**. Many couldn't believe it even when they did. But they did, and instead of swords being converted into ploughshares, swords came out again. Once more, **freedom** would have to be fought for.

15 Patriarchy

ˈpeɪtrɪɑːki noun. m16. . . . 2 A patriarchal system of society or government; rule by the eldest male of a family; a family, tribe, or community so organized. m17. b A system of society or government in which men hold the power and women are largely excluded from it.

In Burma women are completely equal with men. – *U Aung Ko, in* Beyond Rangoon, *1995*

'Patriarchy' is not a word that is alive in the Burmese vernacular. There are a few awkward translations, such as *pogyizothaw-wada*, the ideology (*-wada*) of patriarchal rule. These have contributed little to political debate. But in a manner of speaking, this is the way of patriarchy everywhere. Patriarchal order refuses critique by denying usages with which to denote historically produced situations for men's domination of women. It subordinates them to other topics deserving proper attention: democracy, **federalism**, citizenship, **revolution** and **sovereignty**, topics written about by men. This lexicon is a case in point – as are the selected works in Burmese that make up its tail. That is why it has an entry on patriarchy: not because patriarchy is part of political discourse but because it is not.

One way that patriarchy is denied in Myanmar is via a firm and long-standing insistence that women there are the social equals of men – as U Aung Ko tells his foreign guest in Hollywood's dramatisation of the 1988 uprising, *Beyond Rangoon*. In this scene a male former university professor reassures an American woman that her Burmese counterparts are equal to their menfolk. It is among the film's more accurate characterisations, even if it is factually wrong. Conservative liberals in Myanmar have long shared this view. It has colonial antecedents. British administrators, having discovered the Burmese Buddhist woman, declared that she was less oppressed than women in India or China. They pointed to this as proof not of an enlightened subject society but of enfeebled native masculinity, in contrast to European manhood (see the entry on **Race**). In the 1930s, 1940s and 1950s, new social and political elites recast the colonial story. They ditched racial scientism but promoted the idea that the socially liberated modern woman could stand shoulder to shoulder with her male brethren, even as men continued to dominate public life.

After the military takeover in 1962, the Revolutionary Council and its Burma Socialist Programme Party congratulated women for their contributions to the new socialist economy through agricultural, factory and office work. Though no women occupied positions of importance in government, the men who did emphasised that women and men had equal rights and duties as contributors to the socialist economy. The woman socialist worker was level with her male counterpart. Yet paradoxically, as a group, working socialist women remained the subordinates of men. No platforms existed on which they could collectively stand to demand equal rights.

Patriarchy reached its apotheosis in the decade after 1988. Under the watchful gaze of the State Law and Order Restoration Council, women were reduced to roles for the biological and cultural reproduction of national races. In 1995, without a hint of irony, the junta sent one of its own men to Beijing, where he told delegates at the World Conference on Women that women in Myanmar enjoyed equality with men as an inherent right and had for two thousand years. The government respected them for their part in national **development**. There was nothing more that they wanted or asked for.

Coming to the view that, unlike civil and political rights, the category of women's rights was innocuous and could even be useful, since it would give access to the material and symbolic capital of international organisations, the junta signed Myanmar up to the UN Convention on the Elimination of Discrimination against Women. Its successor, the State Peace and **Development** Council, established the Myanmar Women's Affairs Federation in 2003. The Federation encouraged girls to learn to read and write and pressed women into culturally appropriate activities, like cooking and sewing and childcare, and gainfully employable roles as teachers and nurses and clerks. Under the patronage of military officers' wives and in cooperation with the police force and international organisations, the government ran campaigns to stop violence against women and trafficking to neighbouring countries, among other projects. Through these it could present ideally youthful, poor, rural women and girls with little formal education as vulnerable innocents and virtuous objects for its paternalistic protection.

Whether the women and girls were innocent or virtuous, there was nothing innocent or virtuous about framing them this way. The alleged rape by Muslim men of an ideal typical youthful, poor, rural Rakhine girl with little formal education was what sparked anti-Muslim violence in 2012 and 2013 and anticipated attempted **genocide** five years later. The archetype of an innocent woman in need of patriarchal protection always contains within it the threat of violence towards her opposite: the type of person who would violate her or, more exactly, the type of man who would violate the property relation between her and her presumed menfolk that the archetype affirms.

One of the domains in which paternalistic schemes to define and protect the innocent woman has had its fullest expression is law. This is nothing new. The colonial-era codes that form the backbone of Myanmar's positive law are imbued with Victorian-era morality. Law reports from earlier years are replete with rulings that attend to the status and defence of women and girls cast in terms of ideal types. Concomitantly they denigrate and make vulnerable women and girls who fail to perform moral virtues or fit racial categories that would make them deserving of protection. But in the 2010s the **politics** of law as a shield with which to protect purportedly vulnerable women and girls, and a sword to take to the enemies of **Buddhism**, scaled up. Monks casting themselves as the selfless defenders of women and girls against Muslim men whom they caricatured as sexually depraved predators, led a campaign to pass four laws known colloquially as the *amyozaung ubade*, or roughly, laws to protect one's kind, *amyo*. Dominated by the Union Solidarity and **Development** Party, the legislature passed the laws in 2015, just before the end of its term.

The laws aimed, among other things, at protecting Buddhist women from inter-religious marriage and bigamy. The package was one indication of how in Myanmar men and monks continued in the **reform** era to objectify and class women as vulnerable and in need of their oversight and intervention. That Burmese Buddhist law has long been patriarchal, permissive of bigamy, polygamy and adultery, was elided, as was the underlying conception in the law and cultural practice of marriage as a property relation in which Buddhist men are given exclusive access and ownership rights to Buddhist women. But if it was elided by the law's proponents, it was not missed by its ostensible referent objects: Buddhist women. By the end of the 2020s, the new law on bigamy had reportedly proved popular not among women wanting to separate from Muslims but among Buddhist women wanting to divorce Buddhist men who had had extramarital relationships.

If the 2010s brought with them opportunities for misogynists and chauvinists in the clergy and army to again try to get their way with Myanmar's women, then the decade also brought with it new possibilities to create conditions in which women could challenge and counteract patriarchy. A handful of urban feminist organizations put up a fight. These groups called patriarchy out and celebrated radical feminist struggles and iconoclasts. Alongside them came new efforts to advocate for non-binary people. They were drowned out by larger, better-funded organizations that were less threatening to patriarchy, more cooperative with its institutions. Feminists and non-binary advocates called on the intellectual resources of movements abroad and experiences with patriarchy of activists at home to enliven debate. Other groups got attention for announcing that they would keep doing the same kinds of work as government-organised groups had done under **dictatorship.** They proposed anodyne technical fixes to problems like gender-based violence and trafficking of girls through legislative **reform** and better education. Rather than challenge the gender categories and social institutions of military dictatorship, they built on them.

These groups enlisted many prominent women to their causes: organizers, writers, and legislators who advocated old-fashioned conservative liberal views. Aung San Suu Kyi was their paragon. Though Myanmar's first woman national leader, she ascended to the role dynastically. She is the daughter of a symbol of exemplary masculinity, the national martyr Aung San, founder of its independence army and leader of anti-colonial **revolution**. Throughout the **reform** era his portrait hung alongside hers in people's houses. His face haunted images of hers on calendars, T-shirts and book covers, a ghostly reminder of her paternal lineage, along with the fact that Aung San Suu Kyi's name contains her father's – an unusual practice in a country in which the majority of people have no clan or family names. The matriarch Suu Kyi has used her father's name to her advantage. During her two-decades-long stand-off with the military in the 1990s and 2000s, she characterised theirs as a dispute between siblings. With her resumed captivity in 2021 and the army's redoubled efforts to at last destroy her National League for Democracy, these siblings, like Aung San Suu Kyi and her unremarkable brother, Aung San Oo, might be forever estranged: the one free to act with **impunity**, the other finding **freedom** within.

16 Freedom

လွတ်မြောက်ရေး / lutmyaukye / n freedom; liberation; emancipation.

လွတ်လပ်ရေး / lutlatye / n independence; liberty; freedom.

Saints, it has been said, are the sinners who go on trying. So free men are the oppressed who go on trying and who in the process make themselves fit to bear the responsibilities and to uphold the disciplines which will maintain a free society. Among the basic freedoms to which men aspire that their lives might be full and uncramped, freedom from fear stands out as both a means and an end. – *Aung San Suu Kyi, statement on receipt of the 1990 Sakharov Prize for Freedom of Thought*

In 1990 Aung San Suu Kyi invoked the Universal Declaration on Human Rights to speak of the imperative for freedom from fear, an expression with which she became internationally renowned after being awarded the Nobel Peace Prize the following year. Invoking a Buddhist word for bias or prejudice, *agadi* (from Pali, *agati*), she stressed that democracy depends on the ability to liberate oneself from vices. The quintessential **revolution**, she said, is of the spirit.

This is an idea of freedom as emancipation from internal fetters, so as to be able to take responsibility for oneself and thereby for others. It is an idea that has defined Aung San Suu Kyi's personal struggle against military rule. She has claimed that **dictatorship** has had a debilitating effect on people's sense of duty or responsibility. In the 2010s she exhorted citizens to do the moral work necessary to be able to bear the responsibilities of the **reform** era.

Freedom from fear as the essence of political freedom is a seductive idea. It sets everyone a task that they themselves can accept responsibility to achieve. Everybody has within them the means to self-liberate. However, nothing about this idea is political. This may be why in her Sakharov Prize statement Aung San Suu Kyi preferred to register freedom as a moral problem, a question of emancipation from *bayagadi*, the partiality or prejudice that comes from fear: fear for one's **race** caused by fearsome others; or fear for **Buddhism** because of a perception that Muslim **power** is very great, as Suu Kyi herself put it during a television interview in 2013.

In translation, freedom from fear is freedom as *lutkinye*. This translation correctly registers the original usage's apolitical quality. It is the freedom from danger or sickness that any sentient being seeks, with or without others, with or without political awareness. Politically speaking, freedom is connoted by two related but distinct words: *lutmyaukye* and *lutlatye*. They have a common root, *lut*, which can be coupled with other suffixes to form related words designating pardon, *lutnyein-chanthagwin*, or a loophole, *lutbauk*, an escape hatch through which one passes to get out of a sticky situation. Of the two politically salient usages, *lutmyaukye* denotes emancipation from a condition of enslavement or imprisonment, of pulling or getting free from a state of confinement or oppression. It approximates the idea of liberty as *libertas*, in the Latin, to be exempted or released from bondage or captivity. The other, *lutlatye*, denotes a condition of liberation, in which people speak and act freely with one another, in which they are not subjugated.

The two political usages can refer to the same events or aspirations, viewed from different angles. The first is somewhat like the sense of 'freedom from'; the second, closer to the sense of 'freedom to' or 'freedom for'. So while the fight to throw off the British colonial yoke called for a struggle to obtain political emancipation, *lutmyaukye*, it is commemorated on Independence Day, *Lutlatye Ne*, as the achievement of freedom to decide and act for the future as a sovereign political community.

Both these usages address freedom as an activity that happens in concert and contention with others. In this they differ from Aung San Suu Kyi's. There is nothing in her notion of freedom that precludes these, but nor is there anything in it that makes **politics** possible. Freedom from fear might motivate somebody to act politically, but that need not be the case. People act politically for many reasons. Coupling an apolitical idea of freedom to a political project for freedom does not make the idea itself political.

The distinction is important to dwell on, because it is relevant to the era of **reform** (2011–20) and the revolutionary situation that followed it (2021–2). There are two reasons why. The first is that this conception of freedom puts the onus on the **citizen** to show that they have made an effort at self-improvement. They have to demonstrate that they are capable of taking responsibility for themselves and others and are worthy of recognition as productive members of civil society. Their rights as citizens depend upon their ability to do this – to externalise awareness of their duty to transform themselves in order to contribute to the greater good. No political rights are inalienable. Should anyone fail in their efforts, or not bother to try, they, not those with **power**, have to bear the consequences. Put another way, this is a conception of freedom in which people must first take responsibility for their own lives in order to become worthy of recognition.

Secondly, contrary to the idea that this conception of freedom is opposed to military **dictatorship**, it has affinities with how Myanmar's military presents itself as duty-bound to guard sovereign **power** in the interests of the citizenry. On that account, the responsibility that the army bears for national **politics** arises from the superior attributes, discipline and awareness of duty that entitle soldiers to the freedom they need to act with **impunity** in order to accomplish their great tasks. Army officers also impose standards and place expectations on subjects that they have to meet individually before they are deemed ready to accept political responsibilities. When they fail to demonstrate that they are capable of maintaining these standards, the military reserves the right to intervene and itself shoulder those responsibilities – as, it claimed in February 2021, due to the immorality and inadequacies of the Union Election Commission (see the entry on **Reform**) and the misdeeds of the National League for Democracy and assorted others. In this way, people in Myanmar are kept in the waiting room of history, never self-aware or disciplined enough to bear the responsibilities that come with a free society.

Lutlatye and *lutmyaukye* oppose this situation. So do **politics**, which in certain conditions give way to **revolution**: a collective endeavour for political emancipation. Revolutionaries demonstrate their commitments to others not by trying to make themselves fit to bear responsibilities but by struggling to reconcile various responsibilities that the situation demands they bear together. Political revolutions do not happen when the majority of their participants have readied themselves morally or spiritually. They happen when people interpret the conditions of possibility to act politically and act on that interpretation. Revolutions come, and then they become what people make of them.

References

A Political Lexicon: How Come? – Works Cited

Aye Saung (1989). *Burman in the Back Row: Autobiography of a Burmese Rebel*. Bangkok: White Lotus.

Ball, D., Farrelly, N., Lee, S., and Milner, A. (2007). Languages of Security in the Asia-Pacific [Online]. Canberra: Australian National University. https://asiapacific.anu.edu.au/blogs/languagesofsecurity/ [Accessed 8 December 2019].

Bernstein, J. M., Ophir, A., and Stoler, A. L., eds. (2018). *Political Concepts: A Critical Lexicon*. New York: Fordham University Press.

Blakely, J. (2020). *We Built Reality: How Social Science Infiltrated Culture, Politics, and Power*. Oxford: Oxford University Press.

Charney, M. W. (2009). *A History of Modern Burma*. Cambridge: Cambridge University Press.

Cheesman, N. (2021). Unbound Comparison. In E. Simmons and N. R. Smith, eds., *Rethinking Comparison: Innovative Methods for Qualitative Political Inquiry*. Cambridge: Cambridge University Press, pp. 64–83.

El-Ghobashy, M. (2021). *Bread and Freedom: Egypt's Revolutionary Situation*. Stanford: Stanford University Press.

Fassin, D., and Das, V. (2021). Introduction: From Words to Worlds. In V. Das and D. Fassin, eds., *Words and Worlds: A Lexicon for Dark Times*. Durham: Duke University Press, pp. 1–18.

Gluck, C. (2009). Words in Motion. In C. Gluck and A. L. Tsing, eds., *Words in Motion: Towards a Global Lexicon*. Durham: Duke University Press, pp. 3–10.

Lawson, G. (2019). *Anatomies of Revolution*. Cambridge: Cambridge University Press.

Lezra, J. (2018). Translation. In J. M. Bernstein, A. Ophir, and A. L. Stoler, eds., *Political Concepts: A Critical Lexicon*. New York: Fordham University Press, pp. 208–31.

Lintner, B. (1990). *Outrage: Burma's Struggle for Democracy*. London: White Lotus.

Metro, R. (2011). The Divided Discipline of Burma/Myanmar Studies: Writing a Dissertation During the 2010 Election. *Southeast Asia Program Bulletin*, pp. 9–13.

Myanmar Language Commission (1998). *Myanmar–English Dictionary*. Yangon: Ministry of Education.

Oxford University Press (2007). *Shorter Oxford English Dictionary*, 6th ed. Oxford: Oxford University Press.

Reynolds, C. J. (2014). Keywords for Studying Religion, Power and the Self [lecture]. The Changing Humanities in a Changing World, Chiang Mai University, November 27.

Seekins, D. M. (2006). *Historical Dictionary of Burma (Myanmar)*. Lanham: Scarecrow Press.

Selth, A. (2018). *Burma (Myanmar) Since the 1988 Uprising: A Select Bibliography*, 3rd ed. Brisbane: Griffith Asia Institute.

Sewell, W. H. Jr. (1980). *Work and Revolution in France: The Language of Labor from the Old Regime to 1848*. Cambridge: Cambridge University Press.

Smith, M. (1991). *Burma: Insurgency and the Politics of Ethnicity*. London: Zed Books.

South, A., and Lall, M. (2016). Language, Education and the Peace Process in Myanmar. *Contemporary Southeast Asia*, 38(1), 128–53.

Tilly, C. (1993). *European Revolutions, 1492–1992*. Oxford: Blackwell Publishers.

Walton, M. J. (2017). *Buddhism, Politics and Political Thought in Myanmar*. Cambridge: Cambridge University Press.

Wedeen, L. (2019). *Authoritarian Apprehensions: Ideology, Judgment, and Mourning in Syria*. Chicago: Chicago University Press.

Wells, T. (2021). *Narrating Democracy in Myanmar: The Struggle Between Activists, Democratic Leaders and Aid Workers*. Amsterdam: Amsterdam University Press.

Williams, R. (1983). *Keywords: A Vocabulary of Culture and Society*. London: Fontana.

Recommended English-Language Readings By Entry

1. Politics:

Aung-Thwin, M. (2018). The State. In A. Simpson, N. Farrelly and I. Holliday, eds., *Routledge Handbook of Contemporary Myanmar*. London: Routledge, pp. 15–24.

Cheesman, N. (2016). Myanmar and the Promise of the Political. In N. Cheesman and N. Farrelly, eds., *Conflict in Myanmar: War, Politics, Religion*. Singapore: Institute of Southeast Asian Studies, pp. 353–66.

Crouch, M. (2019). *The Constitution of Myanmar: A Contextual Analysis*. Oxford: Hart, ch. 3

2. Power:

Chambers, J., and Cheesman, N. (2019). Coming to Terms with Moral Authorities in Myanmar. *Sojourn*, 34(2), 231–57.

Gravers, M. (1999). *Nationalism as Political Paranoia in Burma: An Essay on the Historical Practice of Power*. Surrey: Curzon.

Harriden, J. (2012). *The Authority of Influence: Women and Power in Burmese History*. Copenhagen: NIAS Press.

Houtman, G. (1999). *Mental Culture in Burmese Crisis Politics: Aung San Suu Kyi and the National League for Democracy*. Tokyo: Tokyo University of Foreign Studies.

Kawanami, H. (2009). Charisma, Power(s), and the Arahant Ideal in Burmese-Myanmar Buddhism. *Asian Ethnology*, 68(2), 211–37.

3. Dictatorship:

Callahan, M. P. (2003). *Making Enemies: War and State Building in Burma*. Ithaca: Cornell University Press.

Cheesman, N. (2015). *Opposing the Rule of Law: How Myanmar's Courts Make Law and Order*. Cambridge: Cambridge University Press.

Fink, C. (2001). *Living Silence: Burma Under Military Rule*. London: Zed.

Nakanishi, Y. (2013). *Strong Soldiers, Failed Revolution: The State and Military in Burma, 1962–88*. Singapore & Kyoto: NUS Press & Kyoto University Press.

Skidmore, M. (2004). *Karaoke Fascism: Burma and the Politics of Fear*. Philadelphia: University of Pennsylvania Press.

4. Federalism:

Bertrand, J., Pelletier, A., and Thawnghmung, A. M. (2022). *Winning by Process: The State and Neutralization of Ethnic Minorities in Myanmar*. Ithaca: Cornell University Press.

Hmung, S. (2021). New Friends, Old Enemies: Politics of Ethnic Armed Organisations after the Myanmar Coup. Canberra: New Mandala.

Siegner, M. (2019). *In Search of the Panglong Spirit: The Role of Federalism in Myanmar's Peace Discourse*. Yangon: Hanns Seidel Foundation.

South, A. (2021). Towards 'Emergent Federalism' in Post-Coup Myanmar. *Contemporary Southeast Asia*, 43(3), 439–60.

Walton, M. J. (2008). Ethnicity, Conflict, and History in Burma: The Myths of Panglong. *Asian Survey*, 48(6), 889–910

5. Sovereignty:

David, R., and Holliday, I. (2018). *Liberalism and Democracy in Myanmar*. Oxford: Oxford University Press, ch. 4.

Ferguson, J. M. (2021). *Repossessing Shanland: Myanmar, Thailand, and a Nation-State Deferred*. Madison: University of Wisconsin Press, ch. 2.

Maclean, K. (2008). Sovereignty in Burma after the Entrepreneurial Turn: Mosaics of Control, Commodified Spaces, and Regulated Violence in Contemporary Burma. In J. Nevins and N. L. Peluso, eds., *Taking Southeast Asia to Market: Commodities, Nature, and People in the Neoliberal Age*. Ithaca: Cornell University Press, pp. 140–58.

Su, X. (2018). Fragmented Sovereignty and the Geopolitics of Illicit Drugs in Northern Burma. *Political Geography*, 63(1), 20–30.

Woods, K. (2019). Rubber Out of the Ashes: Locating Chinese Agribusiness Investments in 'Armed Sovereignties' in the Myanmar–China Borderlands. *Territory, Politics, Governance*, 7(1), 79–95.

6. Citizen:

Cheesman, N. (2015). The Right to Have Rights. In N. Cheesman and Htoo Kyaw Win, eds., *Communal Violence in Myanmar*. Yangon: Myanmar Knowledge Society, pp. 139–51.

McCarthy, G. (2020). Bounded Duty: Disasters, Moral Citizenship and Exclusion in Myanmar. *South East Asia Research*, 28(1), 13–34.

Nyi Nyi Kyaw (2017). Unpacking the Presumed Statelessness of Rohingyas. *Journal of Immigrant and Refugee Studies*, 15(3), 269–86.

Prasse-Freeman, E. (2023). *Rights Refused: Grassroots Activism and State Violence in Myanmar*. Stanford: Stanford University Press.

Rhoads, E. (2023). Property, Citizenship, and Invisible Dispossession in Myanmar's Urban Frontier. *Geopolitics*, 28(1), 122–55.

Simion, K. (2021). *Rule of Law Intermediaries: Brokering Influence in Myanmar*. Cambridge: Cambridge University Press, ch. 4.

South, A., and Lall, M. eds. (2018). *Citizenship in Myanmar: Ways of Being in and from Burma*. Singapore: ISEAS

7. Race:

Campbell, S., and Prasse-Freeman, E. (2022). Revisiting the Wages of Burman-ness: Contradictions of Privilege in Myanmar. *Journal of Contemporary Asia*, 52(2), 175–99.

Candier, A. (2019). Mapping Ethnicity in Nineteenth-Century Burma: When 'Categories of People' (Lumyo) Became 'Nations'. *Journal of Southeast Asian Studies*, 50(3), 347–64.

Cheesman, N. (2017). How in Myanmar 'National Races' Came to Surpass Citizenship and Exclude Rohingya. *Journal of Contemporary Asia*, 47(3), 461–83.

Ferguson, J. (2015). Who's Counting? Ethnicity, Belonging, and the National Census in Burma/Myanmar. *Bijdragen tot de Taal-, Land- en Volkenkunde*, 171, 1–28.

Roberts, J. L. (2016). *Mapping Chinese Rangoon: Place and Nation among the Sino-Burmese*. Seattle: University of Washington Press.

Thant Myint-U (2020). *The Hidden History of Burma: Race, Capitalism and the Crisis of Democracy in the 21st Century*, London: Atlantic Books.

Venker, M. (2023). Racial Categories, Religious Distinctions: Mixed Buddhists and the Burma Laws Act, 1898–1947. PhD Dissertation. University of Wisconsin–Madison.

Walton, M. J. (2013). The 'Wages of Burman-ness': Ethnicity and Burman Privilege in Contemporary Myanmar. *Journal of Contemporary Asia*, 43(1), 1–27.

8. Buddhism:

Foxeus, N. (2023): Buddhist Nationalist Sermons in Myanmar: Anti-Muslim Moral Panic, Conspiracy Theories, and Socio-Cultural Legacies. *Journal of Contemporary Asia*, 53(3), 423–49.

Frydenlund, I. (2022). Buddhist Constitutionalism Beyond Constitutional Law: Buddhist Statecraft and Military Ideology in Myanmar. In T. Ginsburg and B. Schonthal, eds., *Buddhism and Comparative Constitutional Law*. Cambridge: Cambridge University Press, pp. 198–219.

Nyi Nyi Kyaw (2016). Islamophobia in Buddhist Myanmar: The 969 Movement and Anti-Muslim Violence. In M. Crouch, ed., *Islam and the State in Myanmar: Muslim–Buddhist Relations and the Politics of Belonging*. New Delhi: Oxford University Press, pp. 183–210.

Schissler, M., Walton, M. J., and Phyu Phyu Thi (2017). Reconciling Contradictions: Buddhist–Muslim Violence, Narrative Making and Memory in Myanmar. *Journal of Contemporary Asia*, 47(3), 376–95.

Schober, J. (2011). *Modern Buddhist Conjunctures in Myanmar: Cultural Narratives, Colonial Legacies, and Civil Society*. Honolulu: University of Hawai'i Press.

Schonthal, B., and Walton, M. J. (2016). The (New) Buddhist Nationalisms? Symmetries and Specificities in Sri Lanka and Myanmar. *Contemporary Buddhism*, 17(1), 81–115.

Turner, A. (2014). *Saving Buddhism: The Impermanence of Religion in Colonial Burma*. Honolulu: University of Hawai'i Press.

9. Genocide:

Alam, M., and Wood, E. J. (2022). Ideology and the Implicit Authorization of Violence as Policy: The Myanmar Military's Conflict-Related Sexual Violence against the Rohingya. *Journal of Global Security Studies*, 7(2), 1–18.

Cheesman, N., ed. (2018). *Interpreting Communal Violence in Myanmar*. London: Routledge.

MacLean, K. (2019). The Rohingya Crisis and the Practices of Erasure. *Journal of Genocide Research*, 21(1), 83–95.

Maung Zarni and Cowley, A. (2014). The Slow-burning Genocide of Myanmar's Rohingya. *Pacific Rim Law and Policy Journal*, 23(3), 681–752.

Milbrandt, J. (2012). Tracking Genocide: Persecution of the Karen in Burma. *Texas International Law Journal*, 48(1), 63–101.

Wade, F. (2017). *Myanmar's Enemy Within: Buddhist Violence and the Making of a Muslim 'Other'*. London: Zed.

Ware, A., and Laoutides, C. (2018). *Myanmar's 'Rohingya' Conflict*. London: Hart.

10. Impunity:

Cheesman, N. (2019). Routine Impunity as Practice (in Myanmar). *Human Rights Quarterly*, 41(4), 873–92.

MacLean, K. (2022). *Crimes in Archival Form: Human Rights, Fact Production, and Myanmar*. Oakland: University of California Press.

Verelst, S. (2021). Accountability in Myanmar: A Transformative Stepping Stone? *Global Responsibility to Protect*, 13(2–3), 297–323.

11. Interrogation:

AAPP (2006). Eight Seconds of Silence: The Death of Democracy Activists Behind Bars. Assistance Association for Political Prisoners (Burma).

AAPP (2022). Political Prisoners Experience in Interrogation, Judiciary [sic], and Incarceration Since Burma's Illegitimate Military Coup. Assistance Association for Political Prisoners (Burma).

Cheesman, N. (2016). Reading Hobbes's Sovereign into a Burmese Narrative of Police Torture. *Asia Pacific Journal on Human Rights and the Law*, 17(2), 199–211.

Forensic Architecture (2021). Torture and Detention in Myanmar. https://forensic-architecture.org/investigation/torture-and-detention-in-myanmar.

Ma Thida (2016). *Prisoner of Conscience: My Steps Through Insein*. Chiang Mai: Silk Worm Books.

12. Revolution:

Abuza, Z. (2022). The NUG's Economic War on Myanmar's Military. Washington DC: Stimson Center.

Anonymous (2021). The Centrality of the Civil Disobedience Movement (CDM) in Myanmar's Post-Coup Era. Canberra: New Mandala.

Cheesman, N. (2021). Revolution in Myanmar. *Arena Quarterly*, 8, 60–5.

Frydenlund, I., et al. (2021). Religious Responses to the Military Coup in Myanmar. *Review of Faith and International Affairs*, 19(3), 77–88.

Jordt, I., Tharaphi Than and Sue Ye Lin (2022). How Generation Z Galvanized a Revolutionary Movement against Myanmar's 2021 Military Coup. *Trends in Southeast Asia*, 7. Singapore: ISEAS.

Kyed, H., and Ah Lynn (2021). Soldier Defections in Myanmar: Motivations and Obstacles Following the 2021 Military Coup. Copenhagen: DIIS.

Tin Maung Htwe (2022). Paving the Peaceful Way of Solidarity: The Role of Nonviolent Labourers in Myanmar's Spring Revolution. Canberra: Australian National University.

Zöllner, H. (2009). Neither Saffron nor Revolution: A Commentated and Documented Chronology of the Monks' Demonstrations in Myanmar in 2007 and Their Background. *Südostasien Working Papers* No. 36, Berlin: Humboldt University.

13. Reform:

Crouch, M., and Lindsey, T., eds. (2014). *Law, Society and Transition in Myanmar*. London: Hart.

Egreteau, R. (2016). *Caretaking Democratization: The Military and Political Change in Myanmar*, London: Hurst.

Holliday, I. (2011). *Burma Redux: Global Justice and the Quest for Political Reform in Myanmar*. New York: Columbia University Press.

Lall, M. (2016). *Understanding Reform in Myanmar: People and Society in the Wake of Military Rule*. London: Hurst.

Mark, S. (2023). *Forging the Nation: Land Struggles in Myanmar's Transition Period*. Honolulu: University of Hawai' press.

Mason, D., and Cheesman, N. (2023). Land and Law Between Reform and Revolution. In A. Simpson, and N. Farrelly, eds., *Myanmar: Politics, Economy and Society*, 2nd ed. London: Routledge, forthcoming.

Pedersen, M. (2014). Myanmar's Democratic Opening: The Process and Prospect of Reform. In N. Cheesman, N. Farrelly, and T. Wilson, eds., *Debating Democratization in Myanmar*, Singapore: ISEAS, pp. 19–40.

14. Development:

Aung, G. (2018). Postcolonial Capitalism and the Politics of Dispossession: Political Trajectories in Southern Myanmar. *European Journal of East Asian Studies*, 17(2), 193–227.

Brown, I. (2013). *Burma's Economy in the Twentieth Century*. Cambridge: Cambridge University Press.

Crouch, M., ed. (2017). *The Business of Transition: Law Reform, Development and Economics in Myanmar.* Cambridge: Cambridge University Press.

Ford, M., Gillan, M. and Htwe Htwe Thein (2021). Political Regimes and Economic Policy: Isolation, Consolidation, Reintegration. In A. Simpson and N. Farrelly, eds., *Myanmar: Politics, Economy and Society,* London: Routledge, pp. 105–119.

Jones, L. (2014). The Political Economy of Myanmar's Transition. *Journal of Contemporary Asia,* 44(1), 144–170.

Kenney-Lazar, M., and Mark, S. (2021). Variegated Transitions: Emerging Forms of Land and Resource Capitalism in Laos and Myanmar. *EPA: Environment and Planning A,* 53(2), 296–314.

Kim, K. (2021). Civil Resistance in the Shadow of War: Explaining Popular Mobilization against Dams in Myanmar. PhD Dissertation, Uppsala University.

Kramer, T. (2021) 'Neither War Nor Peace': Failed Ceasefires and Dispossession in Myanmar's Ethnic Borderlands. *Journal of Peasant Studies,* 48(3), 476–96.

McCarthy, G. (2023). *Outsourcing the Polity: Non-State Welfare, Inequality, and Resistance in Myanmar.* Ithaca: Cornell University Press.

Oswald, K., and Tun Myint (2021). Myanmar: Pandemic in a Time of Transition. In V. V. Ramraj, ed., *Covid-19 in Asia.* Oxford: Oxford University Press, pp. 335–48.

15. Patriarchy:

Crouch, M. (2016). Promiscuity, Polygyny, and the Power of Revenge: The Past and Future of Burmese Buddhist Law in Myanmar. *Asian Journal of Law and Society,* 3(1), 85–104.

Hedström, J., and Olivius, E., eds. (2023). *Waves of Upheaval: Political Transitions and Gendered Transformations in Myanmar.* Copenhagen: NIAS Press.

Ikeya, C. (2011). *Refiguring Women, Colonialism, and Modernity in Burma.* Honolulu: University of Hawai'i Press.

Keeler, W. (2017). *The Traffic in Hierarchy: Masculinity and Its Others in Buddhist Burma.* Honolulu: University of Hawai'i Press.

Khin Mar Mar Kyi, M. (2018). Gender. In A. Simpson, N. Farrelly and I. Holliday, eds., *Routledge Handbook of Contemporary Myanmar.* London: Routledge, pp. 381–92.

Sengupta, N. (2015). *The Female Voice of Myanmar: Khin Myo Chit to Aung San Suu Kyi.* Delhi: Cambridge University Press.

16. **Freedom:**

Cheesman, N. (2022). An Experiment with the Island Detention of Public Enemies in Postcolonial Burma. In R. Cribb, C. Twomey and S. Wilson, eds, *Detention Camps in Asia*. Leiden: Brill, pp. 63–81.

Silverstein, J. (1996). The Idea of Freedom in Burma and the Political Thought of Daw Aung San Suu Kyi. *Pacific Affairs*, 69(2), 211–28.

Taylor, R. H. (2002). Freedom in Burma and Thailand: Inside or Outside the State? In R. H. Taylor, ed., *The Idea of Freedom in Asia and Africa*. Stanford: Stanford University Press, pp. 143–181.

Wells, T. (2018). Democratic 'Freedom' in Myanmar. *Asian Journal of Political Science*, 26(1), 1–15.

Select bibliography of works in Burmese

ကလောင်စုံ (၂၀၁၃)။ ခရိုနီ / Crony ၊ ရန်ကုန်၊ ပန်းမျိုးတစ်ရာစာပေ။ [Various Authors (2013). *Crony*. Yangon: Panmyoditya Publishing.]

ကလောင်စုံ (၂၀၁၃)။ ရဟန်းတော်များနှင့် နိုင်ငံ့အရေး၊ ရန်ကုန်၊ အနာဂတ်ကာလ စာပေဆက်ဆံရေး။ [Various Authors (2013). *Monks and National Affairs*. Yangon: Anagatkala Literary Communications.]

ကလောင်စုံ (၂၀၁၃)။ လူမှုရေးနှင့် နိုင်ငံရေးလှုပ်ရှားမှုများ၊ ရန်ကုန်၊ Myanmar Knowledge Society [Various Authors (2013). *Social and Political Movements*. Yangon: Myanmar Knowledge Society.]

ကိုကိုကြီး (၂၀၁၄)။ နိုင်ငံတော်သစ်နှင့် အမျိုးသားအမှတ်သရုပ် အပါအဝင် ဟောပြောချက်များ၊ ရန်ကုန်၊ KQ စာပေ။ [Ko Ko Gyi (2014). *The New State and National Identity: Speeches*. Yangon: KQ Publishing.]

ကိုသန်း (၂၀၁၃)။ NLD နှင့် အစိုးရသစ်တို့၏ ပူးပေါင်းဆောင်ရွက်ရေး အလားအလာနှင့် အခက်အခဲများ၊ ရန်ကုန်၊ နေရီရိစာပေ။ [Ko Than (2013). *Prospects and Difficulties for Cooperation between the NLD and the New Government*. Yangon: Neyiyi Publishing.]

ကျော်မင်း၊ ဦး (၂၀၁၅)။ ရိုဟင်ဂျာသမိုင်းကို ဆန်းစစ်ခြင်း၊ ရန်ကုန်၊ ပညာ–ဧကရီစိုး–စာပေ။ [Kyaw Min, U (2015). *Scrutinising Rohingya History*. Yangon: Panya-egari-zo Publishing.]

ခင်ညွန့်၊ ဦး / မှော်ဝန်းသား (၂၀၁၇)။ ကျွန်တော်ရယ်၊ ထောက်လှမ်းရေးရယ်၊ နဝတနှင့် နအဖရယ်၊ ရန်ကုန်၊ ပန်းမျိုးတစ်ရာစာပေ။ [Khin Nyunt, U /'Hmaw Wuntha' (2017). *MI, SLORC, SPDC and I*. Yangon: Panmyoditya Publishing.]

ခင်ညွန့်၊ ဦး / မှော်ဝန်းသား (၂၀၁၆)။ နိုင်ငံ၏ အနောက်ဘက်တံခါးပေါက်က ပြဿနာ၊ ရန်ကုန်၊ ပန်းမျိုးတစ်ရာစာပေ။ [Khin Nyunt, U /'Hmaw Wuntha' (2016). *The Nation's Western Gateway Problem*. Yangon: Panmyoditya Publishing.]

ချစ်ဝင်းမောင် (၂၀၁၉)။ နိုင်ငံရေးအက်ဆေးများ၊ ရန်ကုန်၊ ပန်းဆွေမွန်စာပေ။ [Chit Win Maung (2019). *Political Essays*. Yangon: Panzwemun Publishing.]

ချစ်သက်ထွန်း / Chit Thet Tun (၂၀၂၂) [2022] ။ ပြည်သူ့ကာကွယ်ရေးတပ်မတော် - ပြည်ထောင်စု တပ်မတော်လား (သို့မဟုတ်) NLD တပ်မတော်လား / People's Defense Forces (PDFs): Federal Army, or NLD Army? Canberra: Australian National University.

စာပေဗိမာန်။ မြန်မာ့စွယ်စုံကျမ်း။ ရန်ကုန်၊ မြန်မာနိုင်ငံဘာသာပြန်စာပေအသင်း၊ အတွဲ ၁ - ၁၅။ [Sape Biman. Encyclopedia of Myanmar. Yangon, Burma Translation Society, vol. 1–15.]

တိုင်းရင်းသားစည်းလုံးညီညွတ်ရေးပါတီ (၂၀၁၂)။ မြန်မာနိုင်ငံ အမျိုးသမီးများ၏ နိုင်ငံရေးလှုပ်ရှားမှု၊ ဒုတိယအကြိမ်။ ရန်ကုန်၊ ရှင်မတောင်စာပေ။ [National Unity Party (2013). Myanmar Women's Political Activism, 2nd ed. Yangon: Shinmadaung Publishing.]

ထက်မြက် (၂၀၁၃)။ NLD ဘယ်လဲ၊ ဘာလဲ၊ ရန်ကုန်၊ မြန်မာ့ခေတ်စာပေ။ [Htet Myet (2013). Whither, Wherefore NLD? Yangon: Myanma Kit Publishing.]

ထန်နိုး၊ သောမတ်(စ်) (၂၀၁၃)။ ချင်းအမျိုးသားတပ်ဦးနှင့် ကျွန်ုပ်၏ တော်လှန်ရေးအတွေ့အကြုံများ၊ ရန်ကုန်၊ ပန်းဝေဝေစာပေ။ [Thangnou, Thomas (2013). The Chin National Front and My Revolutionary Experiences. Yangon: Panwewe Publishing.]

ထွန်းမြင့်၊ ဦး [၂၀၁၇ (၂၀၁၃)]။ ဖက်ဒရယ်မူဆိုတာဘာလဲ၊ ဒုတိယအကြိမ်၊ ရန်ကုန်၊ နေရီရီစာအုပ်တိုက်။ [Htun Myint, U (2017 [2013]). What Is Federalism? Yangon: Neyiyi Book House.]

ဒဂုန်တာရာ (၂၀၁၈)။လွတ်လပ်ရေး၊ နိုင်ငံရေး၊ ငြိမ်းချမ်းရေးနှင့် ဒီမိုကရေစီ၊ ရန်ကုန်၊ စိတ်ကူးချိုချိုစာပေ။ [Dagon Taya (2018). Freedom, Politics, Peace and Democracy. Yangon: Seikkugyogyo Publishing.]

နေစိုးထက် (၂၀၁၇)။ အကဲဆတ်သော ရခိုင်ပြည်နှင့် ပဋိပက္ခများကိုဆန်းစစ်ခြင်း၊ ရန်ကုန်၊ စိတ်ကူးသစ်စာပေ။ [Ne Soe Htet (2017). Fragile Rakhine State, and An Analysis of the Troubles. Yangon: Seikkuthit Publishing.]

နောင်ကျော် (၂၀၁၇)။ ကျွန်တော်က စစ်အာဏာရှင်ငြင်းဆန်ရေးသမား၊ ရန်ကုန်၊ ခဝါလှေမွန်စာပေ။ [Naung Kyaw (2017). I, Military Dictatorship Dissident. Yangon: Kawahlemun Publishing.]

ပန်းသာ၊ နိုင် (၂၀၁၄)။ မွန် နိုင်ငံရေးလှုပ်ရှားမှုသမိုင်းအတွေ့အကြို၊ ရန်ကုန်၊ ဇင်ရတနာဇောစာပေ။ [Pantha, Nai (2014). The Historical Experience of the Mon Political Movement. Yangon: Zinyadanazaw Publishing.]

ဖိုးကျော့ (၂၀၁၇)။ ငါတို့ အနောက်တံခါး၊ ရန်ကုန်၊ ရန်အောင်စာပေ-၂။ [Phoe Kyaw (2017). Our Western Gateway. Yangon: Yan Aung Publishing – 2.]

ဖိုးကျော့ (၂၀၁၄)။ ကိုယ့်သမိုင်း သူ့သမိုင်း နိုင်ငံသမိုင်း၊ ရန်ကုန်၊ သင်းစာပေ။ [Phoe Kyaw (2014). My History, Others' History, the Nation's History. Yangon: Thin Publishing.]

ဖိုးစိုင်း၊ ပြုစု (၂၀၁၆)။ ဒေါ်အောင်ဆန်းစုကြည်၏ ၂၁ ရာစု ပင်လုံမျှော်မှန်းချက်၊ ရန်ကုန်၊ ဂျာနယ်လစ်စာပေ။ [Phoe Sai, ed. (2016). The Hope of Daw Aung San Suu Kyi's 21st-Century Panglong. Yangon: Journalist Publishing.]

ဘစော (၂၀၁၇)။ မြန်မာနိုင်ငံရှိ မူဆလင်လူ့မှုအဖွဲ့အစည်း / *Muslim Society in Myanmar* ၊ ရန် ကုန်၊ ယဉ်မျိုးစာပေ။ [Ba Saw (2017). Muslim Society in Myanmar, Yangon: Yinmyo Publishing.]

မမဦး (၂၀၁၃)။ အရီးပြောမယ် ၂၀၀၈ ခု ဖွဲ့စည်းအုပ်ချုပ်ပုံအကြောင်းကွယ်၊ ရန်ကုန်၊ ပန်းဝေဝေစာပေ။ [Ma Ma Oo (2013). Aunty Tells All About the 2008 Constitution. Yangon: Panwewe Publishing.]

မိုးမခမီဒီယာ (၂၀၁၇)။ မျက်မှောက် ရခိုင်ပြည် မြောက်ပိုင်းအရေး မိုးမခဆောင်းပါးများ (၂၀၀၉ - ၂၀၁၇)၊ ရန်ကုန်၊ မိုးမခစာအုပ်တိုက်။ [MoeMaKa Media (2017). The Current Northern Rakhine State Affair: MoeMaKa Articles (2009–2017). Yangon: MoeMaka Book House.]

မာန်၊ ပြူစု (၂၀၁၆)။ တစ်ခါတုန်းက မြန်မာပြည်မှာ (၁၉၈၈ - ၂၀၁၅)၊ ပထမ+ဒုတိယတွဲ။ ရန်ကုန်၊ မိုးစာပေ။ [Marn, ed. (2016). Once Upon a Time in Myanmar (1988–2015), vols. 1 & 2. Yangon: Mo Publishing.]

မောင်မောင်စိုး (၂၀၁၆)။ တိုင်းရင်းသားလက်နက်ကိုင်များအကြောင်း တစေ့တစောင်း၊ ရန်ကုန်၊ ရန်အောင်စာပေ။ [Maung Maung Soe (2016). Features of National Race Armed Groups. Yangon: Yan Aung Publishing.]

မောင်မောင်စိုး (၂၀၁၆)။ မြစ်ဆုံပြဿနာနှင့် မြန်မာ-တရုတ် ဆက်ဆံရေး၊ ရန်ကုန်၊ မဟာစာပေ။ [Maung Maung Soe (2016). The Myitsone Problem and Myanmar–China Relations. Yangon: Maha Publishing.]

မောင်မောင်စိုး (၂၀၁၉)။ ရခိုင်ပြည်နယ် နိုင်ငံရေးလှုပ်ရှားမှုများ၊ မန္တလေး၊ ဒဿနာရီစာအုပ်တိုက်။ [Maung Maung Soe (2019). Political Movements of Rakhine State. Mandalay: Dandayi Book House.]

မောင်ရက္ခိတ (၂၀၁၅)။ သမ္မာဒိဋ္ဌိလူမျိုး၊ ရန်ကုန်၊ ဂုဏ်ထူးစာပေ။ [Maung Yekkhida (2015). A Race of Right Belief. Yangon: Gôndu Publishing.]

မောင်သိန်းညွန့် (၂၀၁၂)။ မြန်မာ့ဒီမိုကရေစီလွှတ်တော် နိုင်ငံရေးနှင့် ကျွန်တော်၊ ရန်ကုန်၊ သင်းစာပေ။ [Maung Thein Nyunt (2012). The Politics of Myanmar's Parliamentary Democracy, and I. Yangon: Thin Publishing.]

မောင်သွေးချွန် (၂၀၁၅)။ မဘသ၊ ၉၆၉ နှင့် အချုပ်အခြာအာဏာခြံစည်းရိုး၊ ရန်ကုန်၊ မန်းချောင်းစာပေ။ [Maung Thwe Chun (2015). MaBaTha, 969 and the Wall of Sovereignty. Yangon: Mangyaung Publishing.]

မောင်သွေးချွန် (၂၀၁၆)။ အစ္စလာမ်မစ် ဂျီဟာတ်ဒစ်တို့ရဲ့ အကြမ်းဖက်အန္တရာယ်၊ ရန်ကုန်၊ မန်းချောင်းစာပေ။ [Maung Thwe Chun (2016). The Danger of Islamic Jihadist Terror. Yangon: Mangyaung Publishing.]

မျိုး၊ ဦး (၂၀၁၃)။ ဗမာနိုင်ငံ တောင်သူလယ်သမားအရေး လေ့လာသုံးသပ်ချက်စာတမ်း၊ ရန်ကုန်၊ နင်းဆီနီစာပေ။ [Myo, U (2013). A Study of Peasants' Affairs in Burma. Yangon: Ninzini Publishing.]

မြင့်ဇော်၊ မောင် (၂၀၁၂)။ မြန်မာ့လူ့ဘောင်အပြောင်းအလဲအတွက် အရေးကြီးတဲ့ စကားလုံး ၁၀၀၊ ရန်ကုန်၊ ဂျူးစာပေ။ [Myint Zaw, Maung (2012). 100 Important Words for Myanmar's Societal Transformation. Yangon: Gyu Publishing.]

မြင့်သူ (၂၀၁၄)။ မမျှော်လင့်သော ခရီးရှည် (ဗိုလ်ချုပ်ကြီးစိုးဝင်း၏ အတ္ထုပ္ပတ္တိ)၊ ရန်ကုန်၊ ပန်းဝေဝေစာပေ။ [Myint Thu (2014). An Unanticipated Journey: The Biography of General Soe Win. Yangon: Panwewe Publishing.]

မြင့်သိန်း၊ ဒေါက်တာ (၂၀၁၃)။ မြန်မာ့နိုင်ငံရေးနှင့် သမဂ္ဂအဖွဲ့အစည်းများ၊ ရန်ကုန်၊ ဓမ္မသံတော်ဆင့် စာပေတိုက်။ [Myint Thein, Doctor (2013). Myanmar Politics and Unions. Yangon: Dhammathandawsin Press.]

မြတ်သူ၊ တက္ကသိုလ် (၂၀၁၃)။ နိုင်ငံရေးနှင့် နိုင်ငံရေးပါတီ၊ ရန်ကုန်၊ ဟန်သာဆုစာပေ။ [Myat Thu, Tekkatho (2013). Politics and Political Parties. Yangon: Hanthazu Publishing.]

ရဲဘုန်းသိုက်၊ ပြုစု (၂၀၁၃?)။ သတင်းစာဂျာနယ်များကပြောသော အနောက်ဖက်တံခါး (၁)၊ ဦးကျော်သူရ။ Ye Pone Thaik, ed. (2013?). The News Journals on the Western Gateway, vol. 1. U Kyaw Thura.]

ရန်မျိုးသိမ်း၊ ဒေါက်တာ (၂၀၁၃)။ ၂၀၁၅ ခုနှစ်အလွန် NLD ပါတီနှင့် သမ္မတဇာတ်လမ်း၊ ရန်ကုန်၊ စာနဒီစာအုပ်တိုက်။ [Yan Myo Thein, Dr (2013). NLD Post-2015 and the Story of the Presidency. Yangon: Sanadi Book House.]

ရွှေအုန်း၊ ဦး (၂၀၁၄)။ မပြိုကွဲနိုင်သော ပြည်ထောင်စု၊ ရန်ကုန်၊ နေရီရီစာအုပ်တိုက်။ [Shwe Ohn, U (2014). The Unbreakable Union. Yangon: Nayiyi Book House.]

လင်းသက်ခိုင်၊ စုစည်း [၂၀၁၆ (၂၀၁၄)]။ လူထုခေါင်းဆောင်၏ ရဲရင့်သောမိန့်ခွန်းများ	/	Daw Aung San Suu Kyi Speeches ၊ ဒုတိယအကြိမ်။ ရန်ကုန်၊ လဝန်းရိပ်စာပေ။ [Lin Thet Khine, ed. (2016 [2014]). Courageous Speeches of the People's Leader. Yangon, Lawunyeik Publishing.]

ဝင်းဇော်လတ်၊ စုစည်း (၂၀၁၃)။ သတင်းစာတွေ့ပြောတဲ့ ၈၈၈၈ အရေးတော်ပုံ၊ ဒုတိယအကြိမ်၊ ရန်ကုန်၊ တိုးမြှစ်စာအုပ်တိုက်။ [Win Zaw Latt, ed. (2013). The Newspapers on the 8888 Uprising. Yangon: Tomyit Book House.]

ဝင်းတင့်ထွန်း (၂၀၁၃)။ ဗမာပြည်နိုင်ငံရေးပါတီ အဖွဲ့အစည်း အသင်းအပင်းများအညွှန်း၊ ရန်ကုန်၊ ဇင်ရတနာဇော်စာပေ။ [Win Tint Htun (2013). Guide to Political Parties, Organisations, Associations of Burma. Yangon: Zinyadanazaw Publishing.]

ဝင်းတင့်ထွန်း (၂၀၁၄)။ အမှောင်ကြားက ဗမာပြည်၊ တတိယအကြိမ်၊ ရန်ကုန်၊ ပန်းဝေဝေစာပေ။ [Win Tint Htun (2014). Burma in the Darkness, 3rd ed. Yangon: Panwewe Publishing.]

ဝဏ္ဏ၊ အွန်လိုင်း (၂၀၁၉)။ တပ်မတော်ထောက်လှမ်းရေးအရာရှိများနှင့် တွေ့ဆုံခြင်း၊ ရန်ကုန်၊ The Speaker သတင်းဂျာနယ်။ [Wunna, "Online" (2019). Interviews with Military Intelligence Officers. Yangon: The Speaker News Journal.]

သရဝဏ် (၂၀၁၈)။ ရှေ့ရှည်စစ်ပွဲဖြစ်သွားနိုင်သော ရခိုင်ဒေသနှင့် ရခိုင်ဒေသအရေးဆောင်းပါးများ၊ ရန်ကုန်၊ ကံ့ကော်ဝတ်ရည်စာပေ။ [Tharawun (2018). The Makings of a Long War in the Rakhine, and Articles on Rakhine Affairs. Yangon: Kangawwutyi Publishing.]

သရဝဏ် (၂၀၁၄)။ အာဖဂန်နစ္စတန်တွင် ဗုဒ္ဓသာသနာ ကွယ်ပျောက်သွားခြင်းနှင့် အခြားဆောင်းပါးများ၊ ရန်ကုန်၊ ကံ့ကော်ဝတ်ရည်စာပေ။ [Tharawun (2014). The Disappearance of Buddhism in Afghanistan, and Other Articles, Yangon: Kangawwutyi Publishing.]

သက်ဝင်းမြင့် (၂၀၁၆)။ ဒေါ်အောင်ဆန်းစုကြည်အာဏာရှင်လား၊ ရန်ကုန်၊ ကောင်းသန့်စာပေ။ [Thet Win Myint (2016). Is Daw Aung San Suu Kyi a Dictator? Yangon: Kaung Thant Publishing.]

သန့်၊ ဦး။ လာဘ်မိုးဖွေ (၂၀၁၃)။ အရေးအခင်း ပဋိပက္ခများနှင့် ဒီမိုကရေစီတိုက်ပွဲများ၊ ရန်ကုန်၊ လာဘ်မိုးဖွေစာပေ။ [Thant, U / Labmoswe (2013). Civil Strife and Democracy Struggles. Yangon: Labmoswe Publishing.]

သန့်ဇော် (၂၀၁၅)။ နိုင်ငံတော်မှားယွင်းမှု (ဗိုလ်ခင်ညွန့်နှင့် အမျိုးသားထောက်လှမ်းရေး)၊ ရန်ကုန်၊ သင်းစာပေ။ [Thant Zaw (2015). The Wrongness of the State: General Khin Nyunt and National Intelligence. Yangon: Thin Publishing.]

သန်းဝင်းလှိုင် (၂၀၁၆)။ နိုင်ငံတော်၏ အတိုင်ပင်ခံပုဂ္ဂိုလ် ဒေါ်အောင်ဆန်းစုကြည်နှင့် မြန်မာနိုင်ငံရေး အပြောင်းအလဲ၊ ရန်ကုန်၊ ခုနှစ်စဥ်ကြယ်စာပေ။ [Than Win Hlaing (2016). State Counsellor Daw Aung San Suu Kyi and Changing Myanmar Politics. Yangon: Kunitsingyè Publishing.]

သန်းဝင်းလှိုင် (၂၀၁၅)။ သူတို့တိုက်ခဲ့ရသော စစ်နှင့် သူတို့ရှာနေသော ငြိမ်းချမ်းရေး / *The Wars We Fought and the Peace We Look For* ၊ ရန်ကုန်၊ လွင်ဦးစာပေ။ [Than Win Hlaing (2015). The War They Fought and the Peace They Seek, Yangon: Lwin Oo Publishing.]

သန်းဝင်းလှိုင် (၂၀၁၄)။ အာဏာရှင်ဗိုလ်နေဝင်း၏ ဇာတ်သိမ်းခန်း / The Last Days of Gen. Ne Win ၊ ဒုတိယအကြိမ်။ ရန်ကုန်၊ လွင်ဦးစာပေ။ [Than Win Hlaing (2014). The Last Days of Dictator General Ne Win, 2nd ed. Yangon: Lwin Oo Publishing.]

ဟိန်းလတ် (၂၀၁၅)။ အမျိုးဘာသာသာသနာ စောင့်ရှောက်ရေးအဖွဲ့အား လျှောက်ထားမေးမြန်းခြင်း၊ ရန်ကုန်၊ Momentum Book Publishing [Hein Latt (2015). Interviews with the Patriotic Association of Myanmar. Yangon: Momentum Book Publishing.]

အရှင်သောပါက၊ ဒေါက်တာ (၂၀၁၄)။ ဒုတိယညီလာခံ၊ ရန်ကုန်၊ မဇ္ဈိမပဋိပဒါစာပေ။ [Ashin Thawbaka (2014). The Second Conference. Yangon: Mizzima Patipada Publishing.]

အေးသာအောင် (၂၀၁၄)။ ရခိုင်အမျိုးသားရေးနှင့် ပြည်ထောင်စုပြဿနာ၊ ရန်ကုန်၊ ရခိုင်သားကြီးစာပေ။ [Aye Thar Aung (2014). Rakhine Nationalism and the Union Problem. Yangon: Rakhine Thagyi Publishing.]

အောင်စွမ်း (၂၀၁၇)။ စစ်ရေးချို နိုင်ငံရေးပို ဖက်ဒရယ်ဒီမိုကရေစီအရေး တောင်းဆိုလာသည့် ကေအဲန်ယူ၊ ရန်ကုန်၊ Grace Printing House [Aung Swan (2017). The KNU Demands Federal Democracy, and Politics Rather Than War. Yangon: Grace Printing House.]

အောင်ဆန်းစုကြည်၊ ဒေါ် (၂၀၁၄)။ ဒီစကား - ၁၀၀၊ ရန်ကုန်၊ ရွှေပြည်တန်စာပေ။ [Aung San Suu Kyi, Daw (2014). 100 D-talks. Yangon: Shwebyidan Publishing.]

အောင်ဆန်းစုကြည်၊ ဒေါ် (၂၀၁၄)။ အောင်ပွဲမတိုင်မီ၊ ရန်ကုန်၊ ကြယ်နီစာပေသိုက် [Aung San Suu Kyi, Daw (2014). Before Victory. Yangon: Kyèni Publishing Group.]

အောင်မြင့်၊ ဒေါက်တာ၊ ပြုစု (၂၀၁၃)။ ၈၈၈၈ အရေးတော်ပုံနှင့် မန္တလေး၊ ရန်ကုန်၊ ပဉ္စဂံစာပေ။ [Aung Myint, Dr (2013). Mandalay and the 8888 Uprising. Yangon: Pinzagan Publishing.]

အောင်ရှင်၊ မုံရွာ (၂၀၁၆)။ အမျိုးသားဒီမိုကရေစီအဖွဲ့အချုပ် မှတ်တမ်း၊ ဒုတိယအကြိမ်။ ရန်ကုန်၊ ပဉ္စဂံစာပေ။ [Aung Shin, Monywa (2016). Annals of the National League for Democracy, 2nd edition. Yangon: Pinzagan Publishing.]

Acknowledgements

This lexicon had many knowledgeable and interested readers before going to print, especially in its first iteration. I benefited from their advice. Among them I thank Melissa Crouch, Matthew Fenwick, Niklas Foxeus, Iselin Frydenlund, Marija Grujić, Martin Krygier, Nyi Nyi Kyaw, Myat The Thitsar, Rebecca Pearse, Elliot Prasse-Freeman, Craig Reynolds, Elizabeth Rhoads, Ben Schonthal and Alicia Turner. I am indebted to three anonymous peer reviewers for their thoughtful comments and to a number of other Myanmar colleagues whom I cannot name due to the revolutionary situation in their country since mid-2021.

I sketched ideas for the lexicon at sessions of the Australia–Myanmar Constitutional Democracy project in Taunggyi and Yangon during 2018, which colleagues from the University of New South Wales convened with counterparts in Myanmar. I drafted it in 2019–20 while on two fellowships in Japan, at the Center for Southeast Asian Studies at Kyoto University and Ritsumeikan University, Kyoto. At both universities I had generous colleagues and hosts, among whom Yoshihiro Nakanishi, Yoko Hayami and Jun Honna deserve special mention. I am thankful to Noemi Dupertuis for her assistance with accessing Burmese-language books at the CSEAS library. I revised the text in 2022–3 while on a visiting professorship at the Baldy Center for Law and Social Policy, University at Buffalo. Invitations to give talks to the Association of Mainland Southeast Asia Scholars in 2021 and at Arizona State University and York University in 2022 and 2023 presented opportunities to think my way back into the manuscript after I had set it aside due to the coronavirus pandemic and military coup. Thanks to Patrick Jory, Julianne Schober and Alicia Turner for these.

On top of collegiality and office space, Kyoto offered a research stipend and Ritsumeikan a special grant, which I used to buy equipment and materials with which to conduct work on the lexicon. Fellowships in Southeast Asian studies are hard enough to come by these days. The fact that these two universities provided funding on top of being outstanding places to think and read and write is exceptional. In addition to these funds, I have been fortunate to have had an Australian Research Council grant for work in Myanmar and Thailand and to have been on a research team headed by Thongchai Winichakul funded by the Japanese government. Though these grants were not for the writing of the lexicon, I found opportunities during trips they funded to meet people and purchase materials that contributed to the contents of this book.

At the Australian National University, my thinking about how to write a political lexicon of Myanmar benefited from two communities for research and practice. One is the Myanmar Research Centre, which I have directed since 2021. The other is the Interpretation, Method and Critique network, which April Biccum and I convene. I am grateful to everyone involved in both, as well as to the Department of Political and Social Change for its unwavering commitment to grounded, critical research on politics in Southeast Asia.

Thank you also to the Politics and Society in Southeast Asia series editors, Edward Aspinall and Meredith Weiss, for their invitation to contribute, and to Wade Guyitt for the careful copy editing.

Lastly, to every one of my Burmese language instructors, please know that I'd do it all over again. ကျေးဇူးတင်ပါတယ်။

Cambridge Elements ☰

Politics and Society in Southeast Asia

Edward Aspinall
Australian National University

Edward Aspinall is a professor of politics at the Coral Bell School of Asia-Pacific Affairs, Australian National University. A specialist of Southeast Asia, especially Indonesia, much of his research has focused on democratisation, ethnic politics and civil society in Indonesia and, most recently, clientelism across Southeast Asia.

Meredith L. Weiss
University at Albany, SUNY

Meredith L. Weiss is Professor of Political Science at the University at Albany, SUNY. Her research addresses political mobilization and contention, the politics of identity and development, and electoral politics in Southeast Asia, with particular focus on Malaysia and Singapore.

About the Series
The Elements series Politics and Society in Southeast Asia includes both country-specific and thematic studies on one of the world's most dynamic regions. Each title, written by a leading scholar of that country or theme, combines a succinct, comprehensive, up-to-date overview of debates in the scholarly literature with original analysis and a clear argument.